MW00852543

Face of the Lamb

Jesus is Always Right on Time

By

Captain Buddy Bizzell

Capt. Buddy B.

To God be the Glory!

ISBN: 978-0-578-71539-1

Published by Pamela Smalls Ball and SmallStories Publishing.
Printed in the United States of America by Kindle Direct Publishing.

~ *Table of Contents* ~

~ Prayer ~

I humbly pray that God will fill my family and friends with the Holy Spirit. Fill them with Love, Joy, Peace, and Happiness. Thank you God for sending your son to die on the cross at Calvary, to shed His blood to wash away our sins. I pray for your protection for my family and friends.

Thank you for not giving me the spirit of fear, but of Love, of Power, and of sound mind. Thank you for your Grace and Mercy. Thank you for choosing me to be your disciple in Africa, giving me the title of Captain, and allowing me to serve You on the Edisto Palmetto.

I pray You walk hand in hand with me every day. Help me to recognize any lost souls at the crossroads, and witness to them about Jesus Christ; The Way, The Truth and The Life. I pray for discernment to make the right decisions concerning Your plan for my life. I pray that as I follow my heart, You will continue to direct my steps. I pray that whoever reads this book will see the light, and love the light more than the darkness.

Thank You God for saving me and giving me hope and a future. Thank You for surrounding me with godly people to support my walk in Christ. I pray that I continue to stay thirsty for the Word of God all the days of my life, until I come home to be with You. In Jesus Name, I humbly pray. Amen!

~ *Acknowledgements* ~

Many people have influenced my life. My family, friends, co-workers, church family, and my Kenyan family, have all played a supporting role of making me a better person and Christian.

I was very blessed with a loving family. My mom, Linda Bizzell, and stepfather, Ray Bizzell, were two amazing parents. I was taught manners, respect, and how to work hard to have a better life. Thank you, Mom and Dad, for my education, and for always believing in me.

My grandparents were loving people who influenced me in so many positive ways. Both have passed on, but the memories are permanent. My granddaddy loved to hunt and fish. I spent a lot of time on the water with him. My love for the outdoors was instilled in me at a very young age. My grandmother was an inspiration of hard work and her love for people was obvious in her service to her church and mission work.

My cousin, Paul Quinn, has always been like a brother. We have spent many hours on the boat bonding over the years. I want to thank Paul for always being by my side during the good and bad times.

My good friend, Allen Fanning, and his son Braxton, were with me during the night of redemption. They both hold a special place in my heart. They were there to witness the spiritual change in my life. Thank you, God, for putting two Christians by my side at my weakest moment.

Pastor Steve Scott was my pastor at the time of my redemption. Thank you, Pastor Steve, for giving me godly advice, and praying for me when I felt attacked while trying to find my way in the early days of my walk with the Lord.

Pastor Jim Broad, and his wife Joyce, have supported all my visions from the beginning. Thank you both for your prayers, love and support. All of my fundraisers involving food were a success because of your hard work.

Thank you, Bethany Church for supporting my visions. As I've been obedient to serve God in Kenya, your love and prayers have meant so much to my burning desire to serve. Thank you all for the funds, and for supporting many blessings in Kenya, from a church, a church pulpit, and many pairs of reading glasses.

My co-workers were the first to see the change in my life. Because of shift work, I spend more time with them than my immediate family. Thank you for your donations, love and prayers.

My Kenyan family continues to grow. Thank you, God, for making the connections with Swansea First Baptist Church: Pastor Terry Wilder, Mary Corley, and Joe Galloway are just a few of the godly people who have helped mold me into a stronger missionary. I've learned from the best. Dr. Bramwell and Pastor Isaac in Kenya are like family now. I can truly say that part of my heart is in Kenya.

Dr. Ron Rowe of Uttermost Ministries has inspired me to serve God in Africa through building churches. Thank you, God, for making this connection. Dr. Ron has taught me how to do business for God.

These are a few of the many people God has placed in my life to sharpen me, and give me a burning inspiration to serve others with love. God is Love! Love is a language all people understand. Thank you, God, for choosing me and changing my heart to serve others. To God be the Glory! ~Captain Buddy B

~ *Dedication* ~

To my wife Bonnie...you have been my rock since the day we started dating in 1985. My story is your story too. Without your prayers, there would be no story. I thank God for you, and for blessing me with a lifetime Christian partner.

I have so many good memories with you, and I look forward to many more. Thank you for praying for me and never giving up on me. God blessed us with Kristen. It was His timing and His plan for our little family to become complete on September 29, 2006. I'm so proud to call you both my wife and daughter.

Your love and support do not go unnoticed. I know I don't say it enough, but I love you both with all my heart. You are my heart! I want to dedicate this book to you both, because of your love, support and patience toward me. Thank you for being patient with me during my walk with the Lord.

You have heard my story hundreds of times. You have seen me witness to total strangers. You have come to gatherings to hear me speak. I really appreciate both of you walking by my side during this amazing journey. Without your support, there would be no walk and no story. God's plan for my life includes the two most amazing people I know. I love you both to the moon and back!

~ Introduction ~

John 3:17

For God did not send His Son into the world to condemn the world, but that the world through Him might be saved.

I was born July 17, 1967. Andrew Marion Bartley Jr. was my birth name. My first nickname, Bart, was given to me when I was a baby. After my biological father left when I was two years old, I was given my second nickname, Buddy.

My mom remarried three years later, when I was five years old. My stepfather was named Ray Bizzell. At the age of ten, my name was legally changed to Michael Brian Bizzell, but everyone continued to call me Buddy.

I was an alcoholic. I depended on alcohol to soothe my broken life. The stronghold that alcohol had on me affected me, my family, and my friends, in a

1

negative way. I was producing rotten fruit with all of my actions and ways. I was lost and in a very dark place, with no hope in sight. Then, I went on a fishing trip, and a night of redemption turned me around. God changed my heart after six hours of spiritual warfare. I was screaming and begging for his help. Once the night of redemption was over, I became a new creation in Christ!

On March 1, 2014, I became a United States Coast Guard (USCG) Licensed Captain. Today, I am called Captain Buddy Bizzell, and I own and operate Edisto Palmetto Charters LLC on Edisto Island, South Carolina.

I have met many people, and listened to many powerful testimonies on over 300 fishing charters. I love sharing Jesus one charter at a time. I have taken families from over 30 different states on charters. Most families enjoy their first vacation at Edisto Beach. This gives me the opportunity to share my story and the rich history of the island.

Bo Chambers was my first charter in May 2014. His redemption story is almost identical to mine. To this day, we still remain close. We are brothers in Christ, thanks to God's divine appointment.

To this day, I continue to serve the Lord on mission trips and fishing charters. This book is a living testimony of my walk with God over the last eight years of my life. I pray you enjoy my story and are inspired to seek a relationship with Jesus Christ.

~ Face of the Lamb ~

II Corinthians 5:17

Therefore, if anyone is in Christ, he is a new creation; old things have passed away; behold, all things have become new.

It was Spring of 2012. My story was still being written, but all I could see was darkness. I was totally lost. 2011 had been the worst year of my life: my best friend committed suicide, my mother was diagnosed with cancer, and other things in my life were falling apart. I felt like a failure, and I felt like I had lost control. I did not feel worthy.

Every year for the last 15 years, I had been fishing hard for cobia in the month of May. Cobia is a migratory fish. May is a very good time to catch the biggest push of spawning, migratory cobia in the St. Helena Sound near Edisto Island, South Carolina. The

5

state record cobia weighed 92 pounds, and I was looking to break that record.

Every year promised a new challenge, but I was very serious about my fishing. For many years, I had rented the same house on Big Bay Creek on Edisto Island. It was a perfect setup and location for my crew.

In 2012, there was a new challenge. The prime week in May 2012, we found that the house on Edisto Island was already rented. Disappointed, but determined, I found a new place for my crew on Scanawah Island, not far from our fishing grounds of St. Helena Sound. Once everything was booked, I contacted my crew of fisherman friends, and a cousin. We were all set. All we needed was good weather for that weekend.

The weather in early May was shaping up very well and turning warm. During the last week of May, two weeks prior to the fishing trip, I was on my riding lawnmower cutting grass. It was a warm and sunny day.

A flip-flops, shorts, and no shirt kind of day. It was

around 2 p.m., and I had to go to the restroom. I

entered my home and went to the half-bathroom. As I

sat on the commode, I looked down at the tile. Almost

immediately, I saw what looked like a face in the top

left corner of the light-brown colored tile. The face was

about the size of a half-dollar coin.

Closing one eye, I stared at this image. I was

trying to distinguish what I was looking at. Although I

could make out an eye, a nose and a mouth, I wasn't

sure what I was looking at. I stared at the image for so

long that my legs began to go numb from sitting so long

on the toilet.

The next morning, I got up, and immediately

went to the bathroom and looked at the tile...nothing. I

didn't tell anyone about the face I had seen in the tile. I

didn't want anyone making fun of me, or saying something ugly, so I just kept it to myself.

Three days later, I was paying for my gas at the Piggly Wiggly gas station in my hometown of Neeses, South Carolina. Marty Wilson was at the window taking my payment. Marty is a born-again Christian with a powerful testimony. I had known him then for only a short time.

As Marty put my money in the register, I looked down at several missionary pamphlets Marty had placed at the window. I immediately locked in on one of the mission tracks. On the outside cover of the pamphlet was the face of a lamb. I was shocked to see the same lamb's face that I had just seen three days earlier in the tile!

"Marty, can I have this one?" I asked.

He said, "They're all good brother."

"I know, but I want this one." I said.

"Of course you can have it." Marty replied.

I took the mission track with me back to my truck. I opened the pamphlet and read it all. Matthew, Mark, Luke, John...it all went over my head, but I kept it in my console.

A few weeks later, on the eighth night of my fishing trip, I fell to my knees and went through six hours of spiritual warfare with two friends, Allen and Braxton Fanning by my side. The next morning, when it was all over, I rushed out of the house to my truck to get the mission track. I told them there was a message for me in the track. I had been born again. The trees and sky looked different. I had a new heart.

I ran back into the house and opened the

mission track and read it all. This time, it was different.

One verse stood out above all, "Jesus is always right on

time."

Because of God's Grace and Mercy, I was saved.

I became a new creation in Christ. It was the Face of the

Lamb in the tile. God was reaching out to me. He'd

never left me; I'd left him. Thank you, God, for never

leaving or forsaking me. In Jesus name.

~ Buried my Friend at Sea ~

Ephesians 6:10-20

*Finally, my brethren, be strong in the Lord and in the
power of His might
Put on the whole armor of God, that you may be able to
stand against the wiles of the devil.
For we do not wrestle against flesh and blood, but against
principalities, against powers, against the rulers of the
darkness of this age, against spiritual hosts of wickedness
in the heavenly places.
Therefore take up the whole armor of God, that you may be
able to withstand in the evil day, and having done all, to
stand.
Stand therefore, having girded your waist with truth,
having put on the breastplate of righteousness, and having
shod your feet with the preparation of the gospel of peace;
above all, taking the shield of faith which you will be able
to quench all the fiery darts of the wicked one.
And take the helmet of salvation, and the sword of the
Spirit, which is the word of God;
praying always with all prayer and supplication in the
Spirit, being watchful to this end with all perseverance and
supplication for all the saints—
and for me, that utterance may be given to me, that I may
open my mouth boldly to make known the mystery of the
gospel,
for which I am an ambassador in chains; that in it I may
speak boldly, as I ought to speak.*

Guy Glenn was like a brother to me. We first met in 2001 and grew to become very close, because of the things we had in common...mainly fishing. Over the years, our friendship grew stronger on each fishing trip.

Guy grew up on Edisto Island. His dad, Mike Glenn, operated a shrimp boat, so Guy had plenty of experience on the water. We enjoyed one another's company. Our fishing trips were always successful, but we would never keep the fish. We just had fun laughing, and always ended up catching and releasing the fish.

In February 2011, I received the bad news from my mom that Guy was dead. He had committed suicide. I didn't understand. I was mad and angry! Why did this have to happen? I blamed God. I blamed Guy. I asked over and over if there was something I could have done to prevent this from happening. The anger only grew. It was on what I called the last fishing trip, in May 2012, that I buried Guy at sea.

Late in the day, Allen, Braxton and I were fishing on the last day of a week-long fishing trip. This was the last day before my night of spiritual warfare and redemption. This was all God's plan. The plan for my redemption was that night, but my plan was to bury Guy at the end of my fishing trip before returning to the house on Scanawah Island.

We were fishing in a creek by Raccoon Island. Raccoon Island was a familiar island to Guy, because he told me that when he was a kid, that's where his dad would bring the family to crab and fish.

With the music blaring, I told Allen and Braxton to pull up on the island, up to an oak tree hanging out over the water. It was there that I hung a rope in the tree limbs, symbolizing the ropes hanging from my T-top. I looked up into the sky and had a conversation with Guy. I was angry because he had taken his own life.

About three minutes later, when the song stopped playing, I stopped my conversation. I was hurt and I missed him, but I still had no answers. It was only a few hours later, in the house on Scanawah Island, that I was relieved of all the anger and hurt I'd been holding on to. After six hours of spiritual warfare, the next morning at daylight, God had restored my soul. I had been redeemed with a new heart, and a new purpose with visions.

I know now that things happen in life that are out of our control. When these ugly things happen, it is the perfect time to seek God for healing and shelter. At these times, Proverbs 3:5-6 comes to mind:

Proverbs 3:5-6

Trust in the Lord with all your heart,
And lean not on your own understanding;
In all your ways acknowledge Him,
And He shall direct your paths.

For the first time, the anger and hurt were

gone. I felt at peace. Thank you, God, for Your Grace

and Mercy over my life when I have struggled. Thank

You for making me strong and in Your image.

~ *Spiritual Overload: Redeemed* ~

In May 2012, on the eighth night of my fishing trip, at 9 p.m., I was brushing my teeth before bed, and I was spooked at the sink, like something was standing behind me. I asked one of my two friends to lay in bed with me until I fell asleep. Almost immediately, I was at peace and sent my friend back to his room at the end of the hallway.

At 10 p.m., both friends were in separate bedrooms at the end of the hallway asleep. I had to use the bathroom, but after getting spooked earlier, I made it a point not to look into the mirror.

Around 11 p.m., someone in the house screamed, "Buddy!" My friend Allen was awakened. He was the only one who heard the scream. He screamed down the hallway for Braxton, thinking something had happened to me and his son. His screams woke me up. I ran toward Allen in the hallway. By this time, we found Braxton asleep in his bedroom. We were all trying to figure out who called out my name, and why only Allen heard this loud voice. We ended up in the small hallway bathroom. I was afraid to be alone, so as Allen used the bathroom, I stood at the vanity with my back facing the sink. Braxton was in the open doorway. I told them that I could not look into the mirror, but I did.

I turned and looked into the mirror. It was not so much my face, but my eyes that scared me. I fell to one knee and screamed as loud as I've ever screamed. I stood up, with both Allen and Braxton by my side. I started to recall the 23rd Psalms.

Then I looked up at the two rooms at the end of the hallway. The room on the left had an open door, and the light was off. I remember saying that if I went into that room, I was going to hell. I kept saying that I had to go into the room on the right with the door open and the light on.

After entering the room with the light, and closing the door, I fell to both my knees and cried out to God, asking Him to wrap His arms around me and save me. After six hours of spiritual warfare, I walked out of that room with a changed heart.

That night, God gave me three visions...to go to Africa, to be a captain, and to put my story on a CD. All of these visions have since come to pass.

It was during those six hours of spiritual warfare where God and the devil battled for my soul. Those six hours were intense! God buried the heels of my hands into my eyes. I cried out to God to give my eyesight back. I truly felt that if I removed my hands, I would not be able to see.

During the battle, it felt as if two hands were around my neck, choking the life out of me. With Allen and Braxton by my side, we repeated the 23rd Psalms over and over. The louder we said the verses, the more convicted our voices became. It was at those moments when I felt the hands release from my neck, and I was able to stand up. Up and down...up and down...this lasted for hours. Of course, God won the battle!

After breaking all the chains and strongholds in my life, I walked out of the house a new creation in Christ. Pastor Steve Scott explained to me that what I experienced was a "spiritual overload". He said to start seeking the Lord, reading the Bible, and going to church. My visions were overwhelming. As soon as I started seeking the Lord, I found Him. He started opening doors and putting people in place for my visions to come to pass. All I had to do was have faith and continue to be

obedient. To God be the Glory!

~ *Praying with my Mom* ~

The morning after I was redeemed and
restored, I had a purpose to live and visions from God. I
knew I had to go see my mom. She was only a few miles
away on Edisto Beach. I asked Braxton to ride with me
and Allen was going to follow in his truck.

The wind was blowing and gusting very hard,
due to a tropical depression off the coast. I was pulling a
boat so my speed was slow and deliberate. I was going
down this long dirt road, headed toward the main
entrance of the highway, when out of nowhere came a
limb crashing down in front of the truck! Swerving to
miss the tree branch, I looked at Braxton and told him
to hold on.

At the end of the dirt road, I stopped and went
back to tell Allen, who was following, that I was pretty

sure the devil did not want me to go see my mom. I told him I was going to be very careful the rest of the way.

I got back in my truck and told Braxton we needed to start saying the 23rd Psalms over and over on our way to my mom's house, so we did. Halfway to her home, we came upon three vehicles on a curve with double yellow lines. All of a sudden, the third vehicle decided to pass, and ran us off the road. I was able to safely maneuver my vehicle into the ditch.

I looked at Braxton said, "Keep saying the scripture."

We started repeating the 23rd Psalms with power and conviction. Soon, we were going down my mom's long, two-rut, dirt driveway. We came upon a tree that had fell down across the road. I was able to go around it. When we all arrived at my mom's home, I told the guys that I had to go into the house and pray with my mom. One of my sisters, Lori, was staying with my mom for support. Mom had just completed 33 chemotherapy and 15 radiation treatments for small cell lung cancer. I told Allen and Braxton that I had to go and pray with her, and asked them to wait outside. I didn't know how long it was going to take, or even what I was going to say, but I knew God was sending me to pray with my mom.

I entered the house and found my mom and sister sitting at the kitchen table. I walked up to my mom. She was wearing a white housecoat, and her head was bald from the chemotherapy.

I looked at her and said, "Mom, I went through a spiritual warfare last night. Mom I was going to hell, but now I'm going to heaven. My name is written in the Book of Life with the Blood of the Lamb."

"Mom," I said, "You're going to hell."

My mom is a strong Christian woman with strong faith. She answered, "I most certainly am not!"

I asked her to pray with me on her knees. She said her knees hurt, so I grabbed a cushion from the couch and helped her down to her knees. My sister, Lori, interrupted three times. On the third interruption, I asked her to remain quiet and just be a witness.

On our knees, as I held my mom's hands, I asked her to pray with me. As we started to pray, I asked her to repeat after me. But something wasn't right. I soon stopped and asked her to open her eyes and look at me. When she did, I told her that she was not being sincere and that we would try the prayer again. We prayed for God's forgiveness and blessings. When we finished praying, I helped her back into the chair. Looking into her eyes, I told her they were the most beautiful eyes I had ever seen. I felt like I had

gotten my mom back.

As I walked away, I turned back to her and told

her that God wanted her to know that she would live

many more years. Walking out of the house, my sister

Lori followed me with many questions. I know I must

have sounded crazy, but I couldn't answer all her

questions. I only knew that I had done what God told

me to do. As of 2020, my mom is eight years cancer

free! To God be the Glory!

~ Jesus is Always Right on Time ~

Exodus 20: 4-6

You shall not make for yourself a carved image—any likeness of anything that is in heaven above, or that is in the earth beneath, or that is in the water under the earth;

you shall not bow down to them nor serve them. For I, the Lord your God, am a jealous God, visiting the iniquity of the fathers upon the children to the third and fourth generations of those who hate Me,

but showing mercy to thousands , to those who love Me and keep My commandments.

After I left my Mom's house, I had unhooked

the boat, and was headed out of the driveway. Allen

and Braxton had already left for home. I pulled up to

the tree that had fallen across the driveway and

stopped. It wasn't a very big tree, so I grabbed it at the

end, and pulled it around and out of the road.

At this moment, I looked up into the sky with

my arms stretched over my head, and asked God if all

29

this happening to me was real. I asked God if this was real, could He show me a sign. All of a sudden, a big white bird flew from one white cloud straight over my head, and disappeared into another cloud in the blue sky. My mouth fell open. I walked over to my truck and asked God to ride home with me and He did.

On the way off the Edisto Island, I became very sleepy. I was approaching an AME Baptist church. It was a church that I had pulled over to rest at many other times, but this time was different.

As I pulled into the drive, I noticed the sign said, "Jesus is always right on time." I was shocked! This was also the phrase that jumped out at me when I had read the mission track with the lamb's face earlier that morning. I knew it was important so I wanted to write it down.

I found a pen and opened my tide log book to right this message down. I began to write, "Jesus is always…" and when I started writing the "R" in "right", I fell asleep and my pen ran off of the page. I don't know how long I was asleep, but when I woke up, and removed my sunglasses, I turned my log book to that day's date, Sunday, May 28, 2012, and this is what I'd written, "Jesus is always right on time. Not Guy G."

I didn't understand why I wrote this, but later, God revealed to me what it meant. I was putting my friend first before God. I loved our friendship dearly, and would do anything for Guy. This was the problem. God wants us to put Him first in all that we do. We should give God all the praise and glory for the little things, as well as the big things. Jesus is always right on time! There is nobody else. Only Jesus! We should worship God and nothing else.

Acts 1:7

And He said to them, "It is not for you to know times or seasons which the Father has put in His own authority.

II Peter 3:8

But, beloved, do not forget this one thing, that with the Lord one day is as a thousand years, and a thousand years as one day.

Ecclesiastes 3:1

To everything there is a season,
A time for every purpose under heaven:

~ Bird Dog ~

As I was leaving the Edisto Island the morning after redemption, I saw a man walking on the shoulder of the road. After passing him by, I was prompted by the Holy Spirit to turn around and pick him up. It was obvious he was walking to the local convenience store just down the road. I pulled up and offered him a ride.

After getting into my truck, and taking him home, I realized I was sitting in the driveway of my best friend, Guy Glenn's house. Guy's suicide in 2011 devastated me and the whole community. I looked at the man and told him that Guy was a good friend of mine. The man told me that he missed Guy every day. I saw a teardrop roll down his left cheek.

As we turned our attention to the driveway, a liver brown and white bird dog came out of nowhere, stopping a small distance from my truck. The dog cocked his body into a pointed position.

I looked at the man and asked, "Have you ever seen that dog before?"

He said, "I've lived here all my life, and I've never seen that dog before."

I realized the dog was pointing at my truck, and I asked the man if he thought the same. He said, "Yes sir."

The bird dog came out of his locked position, moved over, and then locked himself back into a pointed position for a second time.

Not knowing or understanding the meaning of this, I asked many people, including deacons and pastors, if they knew what this symbolized. None of them knew the answer.

I had recently left my mother's home earlier that morning after praying with her. I stopped at the end of her driveway, and asked God if what I was experiencing was real, for Him to show me a sign. The first sign He showed me was a bird, and the second sign He showed me was a bird dog. I didn't understand what these signs meant.

After six months with no answers, I decided to google "bird dog". Before I googled, I asked God to reveal the answer to me. When I googled "bird dog", a page-long description of a bird dog popped up. I read the information and in the last paragraph I found the answer. It said, "When a bird dog locks in on a bird, a rabbit can run by, but he will not chase the rabbit, he will stay locked in on the bird."

There was my answer! God was telling me to stay locked in on Him, and not to chase the temptations of the world, such as alcohol, gambling, and drugs. Jesus

Christ is the way, the truth, and the life.

God speaks to us through dreams, visions and

signs. If we continually seek Him and stay in the Word,

we will recognize His calling on our life. Pray for

discernment and let the Holy Spirit guide your steps. To

God be the Glory!

~ 9-1-1: Visions in a Mirror ~

When I arrived home the evening after going through spiritual warfare and being redeemed, I was so excited to share my story. I can only imagine how crazy it must have sounded to my wife. I'd had a spiritual overload from God, and He had given me a new heart with visions. I was a new creation in Christ. Just like a baby!

I didn't know how to explain what had happened to me, but I knew I had a purpose to live. I told these stories of visions to my wife, and explained that everything was going to be okay. I wanted to live, but I was going to live serving God. Being the loving wife that she is, she was concerned because I sounded crazy. She called 9-1-1, and told them I was in the bedroom. She was right...I was in the bedroom, getting ready to go to sleep.

Everyone came to my house except for the fire department. I was looking into the mirror and all of a sudden, I could see hundreds of animals. I wasn't sure, but I thought God was showing me all the animals in Heaven. However, it wasn't all the animals in heaven. I found out three years later on my first mission trip to Kenya, that God was giving me a glimpse of where He was taking me in Africa. He was taking me to a place where there were zebras, rhinos, giraffes, and lions.

On that trip, our mission team traveled to the Mara Safari, when we came over this high ridge. I looked across the plains and all I could see were animals; the same vision God had shown me in my bedroom mirror.

That night, when the knock on my door came, I sat at the end of the bed. The door opened with the police, SWAT team, and paramedics all standing there. I invited them in. The paramedics put the blood pressure cuff on my left arm. My blood pressure was a perfect 120/80. They asked me what I had been drinking, and I said water. They asked me if I smoked, and I said that I didn't smoke. They asked me if I took pills, and I answered that I didn't take pills. They decided that they had asked enough questions. However, they handcuffed me after I told them that I was full of God. I was transported to the Orangeburg Regional Medical Center. After being sedated and getting a good night's sleep, I was admitted to the Rose Centre, an inpatient psychiatric unit within the medical center.

Dr. Rose Lawson entered the room for my initial meeting. God was already lining things up, but I didn't know this at the time. He will put the right people in your life to get the best results for you. You just have to believe and be faithful. Dr. Lawson asked me to tell her what happened. First, I asked her if she was a Christian, and she said yes.

After sharing my story of redemption, I asked her if I was crazy. She said no. I asked her if I was a schizophrenic. She said no. I asked her if I was bipolar. She said no.

I asked, "Okay then...what is wrong with me?"

She said, "You had a nervous breakdown. You fell to your knees and called out to your God. Now it's between you and your God. I'm just your doctor."

I exclaimed, "Praise the Lord!"

I asked her how long I would be there, and she said five days. I was out in four days. God took nothing away from me, but He gave me everything, Love, Joy, Peace and Happiness.

When I was in the world, I would pray. I would also look in the Bible for answers and direction. The problem was, I had no faith. I didn't know how to pray and believe. My relationship with Jesus Christ didn't exist. I would do it all on my own.

When searching the Bible for answers to my problems, I would randomly open the Bible to a scripture, hoping for an answer. If I didn't like the scripture or what it said, I would just keep turning the pages until I found a scripture that I felt was appropriate for my circumstances at that moment.

I've heard preachers or Christians say, "I am in the world, but not of the world." I never understood that statement before, but now I do.

Shortly after my fishing trip of redemption, I was sitting alone in my living room, praying and talking to God. I was asking for guidance. Holding the Bible in my lap, I prayed that I would open it to a scripture that would lead me in a direction of joy, peace and happiness. I needed a scripture to give me some direction.

After praying and asking God for His help, I opened the Bible to the book of Job. I began to read the story of Job and how he had lost everything, but in the end of his tribulation, God restored his life to more than he could have ever dreamed of. I felt the love and guidance from God at that moment.

It had only been two weeks and I was reading the Bible for the first time, but this time was different. This time, I didn't just flip through the pages. I prayed and asked God for direction. The book of Job gave meaning and purpose to my life. Never lose faith in God. Always give God all the praise and glory in all situations, good and bad. This was the first time I truly understood the meaning of, "I am in the world, but not of the world."

God began to mold me. When I pray now, I believe! I have faith that God is in control of every circumstance and situation in my life. I can now say that, "I am in the world, but not of the world."

The story of Job teaches us to never lose faith, no matter how bad the storms get. Storms are temporary, but God's grace and mercy are permanent.

~ The Addiction Broken ~

James 1:12-18

Blessed is the man who endures temptation; for when he has been approved, he will receive the crown of life which the Lord has promised to those who love Him.

Let no one say when he is tempted, "I am tempted by God"; for God cannot be tempted by evil, nor does He Himself tempt anyone.

But each one is tempted when he is drawn away by his own desires and enticed.

Then, when desire has conceived, it gives birth to sin; and sin, when it is full-grown, brings forth death.

Do not be deceived, my beloved brethren.

Every good gift and perfect gift is from above, and comes down from the Father of lights, with whom there is no variation or shadow of turning.

Of His own will He brought us forth by the word of truth, that we might be a kind of firstfruits of His creatures.

Alcoholism is an addiction that had a stronghold on my life. I was a functioning alcoholic. The drinking was not a problem until it began to control my life. My drinking also affected my family and friends.

Twenty years ago, I wanted to pursue my dream of becoming a captain. I purchased a $50 book, and registered for a $1,000 class called Sea School. The week the class was scheduled, the instructor became ill, and the class was cancelled. I was disappointed. Looking back now, I realize that I would have failed if I had become a captain and started a business at that time in my life. Alcohol would have been my downfall.

Now that I'm running a successful charter business, I know that there is no way I would have succeeded 20 years ago. God was protecting me. Sometimes He closes doors to protect us and this was definitely one of those times.

On January 7, 2013, I came home drunk for the last time. Even though I had been born again in May 2012, I had yielded to the temptation of alcohol once again. It was controlling my life, but this time was different.

I realized that I was about to lose everything – my wife, my home, my child, and my job. My pastor, Steve Scott, told me that I needed to stop drinking, start reading the Bible, and start going to church. For the first time, I knew that I needed to try a different way...God's way. I asked Jesus for help to overcome my addiction to alcohol. I told my wife that I would never drink again.

"Well," she said, "You've been saying that for twenty years. We'll see!"

A few weeks later, I was sitting in my living room watching TV. My wife was in the kitchen. It had been two weeks since my last drink. A Miller Lite commercial came on TV. As the beer was being poured into a glass, I asked my wife to come into the living room. When she came into the room, I told her to look at the TV.

She did, then she said, "I guess you want a beer."

I said, "Believe it or not, that looks like urine to me."

Normally my reaction or response would have been to go get a beer out of the fridge. This time was different. I knew it, but I had to prove it.

Over the next several months, I was becoming stronger over my addiction. It was May 2013, and my annual fishing trip was coming up.

My wife said, "We'll find out if you've really quit drinking when you go on this week-long fishing trip."

I knew the temptation would be great and I was worried. I reached out to Pastor Steve. I asked him to pray for me, so that I would not be overcome with the temptation to take a drink.

Pastor Steve said, "Brother, this is what I want you to do. Each time someone hands you a drink of alcohol, put it down, and say, 'I trust in the Lord.' Each time you repeat this, you'll get stronger and stronger. Eventually, by the end of the week, you will have overcome the temptation to drink alcohol. Trust in the Lord."

After I spoke with Pastor Steve, I felt better. On the way to Edisto Island, South Carolina, to start the fishing trip, I stopped by the church that I had stopped at in 2012. This was the same church where I saw the sign, "Jesus is always right on time." I was talking to God and asked Him to show me a message that would help me to not drink on this fishing trip. I pulled into the church yard and the sign said, "Trust in the Lord." This was the same message Pastor Steve had just told me. I was ready for battle!

Arriving at the fish house, I was greeted at the door by one of my good buddies.

"Here," he said. He was holding two quarts of moonshine, and handed them both to me. One was blueberry flavored, and the other was apple pie flavored. I took the jars of moonshine, one in each hand, and walked over to the kitchen table.

As I placed each jar on the table, I said, "I trust in the Lord."

By day three, it was obvious to my fishing crew that something was different about me. I was not drinking any alcohol. I told them not to worry and that everything was absolutely fine. They were still concerned.

By the end of the week, I was still sober. My friends were very proud of me, and happy for me. One of them even told my wife that he would have never believed it if he hadn't seen it with his own eyes. Buddy Bizzell fished for one solid week without drinking. It was a huge compliment and I graciously accepted it.

With the help of Jesus Christ, my addiction to alcohol was broken. God immediately started opening doors for me no man could close. He also started closing doors to protect me. My dreams and visions started to take shape.

As soon as I started walking the walk, instead of talking the talk, my journey with the Lord was put into action. My actions started to speak loudly each time I was obedient to God. Within a few months, I was walking in God's favor, totally sober. To this day, I remain sober, and I have no desire to drink alcohol ever

again. I trust in the Lord! To God be the Glory!

~ My Faith is Tested ~

Luke 1:37

For with God nothing will be impossible.

One day, in 2013, I noticed a small bump on my left shoulder. I assumed it was a pimple, and thought no more about it. A few days later, I realized that the bump was different than a normal pimple. The bump was about the size of a pea, and had the texture of the skin of a baby mouse. I still was not that concerned, but I did ask a few family members to check it out for me. They each said it looked like a cyst.

Over the next year, the cyst became larger, and was now the size of a marble, with the same smooth texture as before. However, it had become sensitive to the touch, sometimes hurting when my shoulder would bump into a door or a doorway.

I scheduled an appointment with the local dermatologist. After a short visit, he told me not to be concerned, that it was only a cyst, and it would eventually go away. I was relieved with the good news! I told my wife not to worry, because the doctor said that it was only a cyst.

One year later, the cyst had gotten extremely sensitive to the touch, sometimes taking my breath away when I bumped my shoulder on anything solid. My wife insisted I go back to the doctor, but this time she scheduled me to see a different dermatologist. I decided to go get a second opinion. When the new dermatologist came into the room, she immediately noticed the cyst on my left shoulder.

She said, "This is not good. We need to get this checked immediately."

I calmly explained to her that I had already had it checked a year earlier, and was told that it was only a cyst.

She gave me a serious look and said, "This could take your life."

Well, that got my attention! I sat up straight, and told her that I was not afraid, and that my name was written in the Book of Life with the blood of the lamb. She left the room to get a nurse to assist her with the biopsy of the cyst. I immediately fell to my knees and prayed to God for healing in the name of Jesus Christ. Almost immediately, a feeling of peace came over me. She returned to the room, and they took the sample.

Three days later, she called me with the results. I had Leiomyosarcoma muscle cancer. Leiomyosarcoma is a rare type of cancer that affects smooth muscle tissue. She told me it needed to be removed. I calmly responded that I was busy, and could not do the surgery until fall of that year.

She said, "You may be dead by then."

Not that really got my attention! Four days later, I had the surgery, and the cyst was successfully removed. I was blessed! No chemotherapy or radiation treatments were needed! I ended up with a nasty scar on my left shoulder, because the tissue around the cyst was removed down to the muscle. The cancer was not in my shoulder muscle, so I didn't lose any motion in my left arm. I was blessed with a full recovery!

For the first time after my redemption, my faith was tested. I remember my family being very concerned and worried during this time. I told my wife that after my prayer in the doctor's office, I felt at peace. I knew in my heart God was in control. I also let my wife know that I felt like God had too much work for me to do, and it was not yet time for me to go to heaven. I was trying to comfort my wife, but I was very confident in my belief.

My faith had been tested and I was giving it all to God. I had prayed and believed in His healing over my body. I believed in Him, and did not fear. I was protected and healed in the name of Jesus Christ. I use this personal lesson in my life often when I'm praying about a situation that seems impossible. Nothing is impossible with God!

~ Confirmation from God ~

John 3:16

For God so loved the world that He gave His only begotten son, that whoever believes in Him should not perish but have everlasting life.

May 28, 2014 was exactly two years to the day after my redemption. In the beginning of my charter business, Edisto Palmetto Charters, my name was not in the public eye, nor on any social media outlets. My very first charter had been cancelled, so there was nothing on my books.

On May 26, 2014, a good friend from Edisto Island, Cubby, introduced me to one of his friends, Dan Corley. Dan's brother, Chris Corley, ran a successful shrimp boat on the island. Dan knew that I was anxious to book my first trip, and just needed a chance to get my name out there. I gave Dan my information.

Later that evening, Dan called with the name of two potential fisherman who wanted to split the cost of a trip. I was excited and grateful. I told him to give them my information so they could give me a call. Bo Chambers and Paul Threatt each called. I booked my first trip for Friday, May 30, 2014.

Due to a recent surgery on my left shoulder, I needed a first mate. The surgery was to remove a small tumor called a leiomyosarcoma, which is a form of muscle cancer. I had 12 stitches from surgery, so I asked my good friend, Rick Fogle, to assist me. He was glad to help, but wanted to make sure it was an inshore trip, because he doesn't like to go offshore. I told him it was an all-day inshore trip for shark and cobia.

I was so excited the morning of the trip. I wasn't excited about catching fish, as much as I was excited about sharing my testimony on the fishing trip for the first time.

Waiting at my boat on the dock that morning, I spotted my first client walking toward the dock. It was Bo Chambers.

He approached me, extended his hand, and introduced himself.

"Hi, I'm Bo Chambers," he said. "Here, I have a coin to give you."

I looked down and he handed me a Christian coin. One side said, "Where will you spend eternity?" The other side had the John 3:16 scripture printed on it.

I looked up at him, teary-eyed, and said, "Brother, I've got a testimony for you."

Paul Threatt was soon aboard, and we left for the St. Helena Sound. It was a beautiful day, and a very successful fishing trip. Paul landed a 30-pound cobia, and Bo landed a 65-pound black tip shark.

On the way back to the dock, Bo offered to cook for my fishing crew that evening. It was totally amazing how good the fish turned out. We found out that Bo was a master chef and knew how to cook. We had charcoal-grilled black tip shark for dinner.

As I spent time with Bo that evening, he eventually shared his testimony. It was such a powerful testimony. He said he had been running hard for a couple of weeks, totally lost. He came home one night, and passed out. The next morning, he couldn't remember much, but fell to his knees and cried out to God for over six hours to save him. He said that was when his life changed, and he'd been handing out the Christian coins since his deliverance. I was amazed and shocked!

Now I knew why my very first charter got cancelled. God wanted Bo Chambers on my boat! Our testimonies were almost identical. I'd also fell on my knees, and cried out to God for six hours during my night of redemption.

God was giving me confirmation through my new brother in Christ, Bo Chambers, and now we have grown to be close friends. He has been fishing with me many times since then, but not as a client. He's always my first mate when he steps on the Edisto Palmetto. Thank you God for making this connection, and giving me confirmation on my first trip. To God be the Glory!

~ Kenya Connection: God's Way ~

On the way to work the night shift, I was listening to 99.9 WUCC Christian radio station. The South Africa pastor was sharing a powerful message. The more I listened, the more intense the message became. He was speaking about being a missionary in Africa, and being obedient to your calling. The timing was perfect! It was God's timing.

It was 2013, not long after I had been born again on Scanawah Island in May 2012. I felt like God was preaching to me. I was overcome with emotion and the Holy Spirit. The tears started flooding down my face. I had to pull over and collect myself. I couldn't see enough to drive. I finished listening to the sermon, and there was a number to call at the end of the message. I called the number, and it was an automated answering machine, so I knew I would have to call the radio station the next day. I could not wait!

I arrived at work, and the first person I saw in the office was my manager, Brian Ashe. I had to share my experience about the message on the radio. I told him that I knew without a doubt that I was going to do mission work in Africa. I just didn't know when. I asked him what he thought.

He said, "Well, I've been working here over 30 years, and you're the second person to tell me that."

I asked, "What happened to the first person?"

He said, "She became a missionary."

We both laughed, but I knew it was going to happen. That night at work, I studied a map of Africa. I was going! I thought about traveling somewhere close to the water since I love to fish. I just didn't know where.

The next day, I called 99.9 WUCC radio station, and spoke with the co-owner, Pastor Steve Hall. He invited me to come meet with him and talk about the sermon and message I had heard on the radio. My visit with him went well. I shared my story, but the type of mission work the South African preacher was looking to do didn't fit my life at the time. I was discouraged, but I still knew I was going eventually.

I had no idea God was already lining up things in my favor. Just a few weeks later, I was driving through Swansea, South Carolina, and the church sign at Swansea First Baptist said, "Pray for our Kenya Mission Team." I saw this sign, and immediately, I felt the Holy Spirit prompt me to turn toward the church and ask for some more information about the mission trip, but I was in a hurry and kept going down Highway 321. I had no idea at the time that God was leading me to my Africa connection.

It was now January 2014, and it had been very cold for several days in a row. I ended up with a busted water pipe in my upstairs bathroom. I was able to fix the pipe that was shattered, but the damage was tremendous. The water been running over seven hours and ended up costing over $20,000 to repair all the damage. To make things worse, I rolled my left wrist while fixing the pipe.

The next morning, I was in pain. I left for North Medical Center to get an x-ray, but I was turned away because I didn't have an appointment. I went to Orangeburg, only to have the same results. I decided to drive toward Columbia until I could find an urgent care center x-ray my wrist. I ended up at Swansea Urgent

Care. There I met Mrs. Mary Corley. I will never forget her. She was taking my information, and I noticed pictures on her desk from Africa, as well as many little souvenirs. I told her that I had been called to go to Africa, and that I was hoping to go one day.

She immediately stopped, looked at me, and said, "I've been six times."

She gave me her pastor's number and insisted I call him when I left. After the x-ray, I left with a soft cast on my cracked wrist. I thanked God for not cracking my head. I called Pastor Terry Wilder, and he invited me to come and visit. I walked into his office at Swansea First Baptist Church, where the sign, "Pray for our Kenya Mission team," stood outside in front of the church.

I could feel the Holy Spirit as I looked at all the pictures from Africa on his walls. I introduced myself and asked if he believed in divine intervention.

69

He said, "Absolutely."

An hour later, after sharing my visions and testimony, he gave me the dates for their next mission trip, September 2015. I was so excited! I told him to put my name on the list and I would get the details later.

Finally, I knew when I was going to Africa! I thanked God again for not cracking my head. He sure did get my attention the second time! He had it planned all along; I just had to be obedient.

I was definitely learning to recognize when the Holy Spirit was trying to get my attention. I immediately called my wife to give her the great news. She had been asking when I was going to Africa. I could only tell her that I would know when God told me. Now I finally had all the details. I've been to Kenya three times now on medical missions...2015, 2017, and 2019. To God be the Glory!

~Perfect Will of God: First Medical Clinic in Kenya~

Acts 1:8

"…But you shall receive power when the Holy Spirit has come upon you; and you shall be witnesses to Me in Jerusalem, and in all Judea and Samaria, and to the end of the earth."

On our 2015 Kenya Medical Mission, Matunda Baptist Church was the location of the first medical clinic. My very first Kenyan experience was a medical clinic put together by Swansea First Baptist Church. For more than 15 years, they had visited Kenya, bringing food and medicine. Pastor Terry and his team had paved the way with relationships and connections in Kenya to make the greatest impact during our two-week mission trip.

As we arrived at Matunda Baptist Church, we were greeted by Pastor Isaac. The tents outside the church were already overflowing with people, some of whom had spent the night, hoping to get some medicine or treatment from a doctor. Pastor Terry had already bought food and medicine, and hired four doctors with several nurses to accompany us to each clinic. Everything and everyone was ready to serve the Kenyan people.

As we exited our white vans, called matatus, we were greeted by joyful people welcoming us all. There were over 30 little kids gathered around, singing a welcome song in Swahili. It was powerful! I didn't know the words, but the smiles and body language were overwhelming. I could feel the Holy Spirit! It was like electricity running through my body from head to toe. I looked at the person next to me and told them there was no other place in the world I was supposed to be. I felt a perfect peace I had never felt before. I was in the perfect will of God. I knew I was supposed to be there,

helping and sharing about Jesus.

God has called us to go to the ends of the earth

and share the gospel. Not everyone can go to Africa, but

you can pray for the mission teams that do.

Captain Buddy Bizzell sharing Jesus with the people of Kisii, Kenya during a
medical clinic. (Kisii, Kenya, 2015)

~ Golden Tots Preparatory School ~

There is an awesome school, located in Kitale, Kenya, called the Golden Tots Preparatory School. This is a school of orphans, run by Dr. Bramwell and his wife, Abigail, and it is home to over 200 children.

Pastor Terry Wilder met Dr. Bramwell on a mission trip over ten years ago. They became friends, and Swansea First Baptist Church has been supporting the school ever since, through donations, purchasing school buses, and building dormitories.

On my first mission trip in 2015, I met Dr. Bramwell and his wife, and I visited the school of orphans. Each time I return to Kenya, I visit this little school, and I fall more in love with it every visit. I've visited the Golden Tots Preparatory School three times now, and each time, the children greet us at the entrance gate to the school, with big smiles, laughter, and lots of singing and dancing. My favorite song that they sing is a welcoming song called "Fishers of Men". I love getting them to sing this song on each visit. It is truly a heart-warming experience for me to visit and spend time with these children. Their positive attitudes, smiles, and energy always inspires our mission team.

Captain Buddy Bizzell handing out candy and telling stories about the different types of fish caught on his boat, The Edisto Palmetto. (Golden Tots Preparatory School, Kitale, Kenya, September 2015)

Handing out candy is one of my favorite things to do when I'm there. They love lollipops! During my first visit in 2015, I remember asking if there was anything that I could do for the children.

I was humbled when they responded, "Yes sir. Could you write us letters?"

I thought for a second and realized that a lot of letters would be needed for the amount of children that attended this school.

Then I said, "I'll get my little girl's third grade class at Orangeburg Preparatory to write the letters, as well as her Sunday school class."

They were so excited and happy! The letters took a couple of weeks to be delivered, but it was a huge success! I loved connecting the children of Kenya with the children of Orangeburg through letters, and

creating lifelong relationships!

Captain Buddy Bizzell showing pictures of the different types of fish he caught on the Edisto Palmetto. (Golden Tots Preparatory School, Kitale, Kenya, September 2015)

I immediately fell in love with the children at

the Golden Tots Preparatory School. They were always

so happy and full of energy, and thirsty for the word of

Jesus Christ. My most memorable moments are sharing

Jesus, and showing the children pictures of big fish. Seeing their reactions was priceless!

The experiences of visiting the Golden Tots Preparatory School has humbled me, and given me an urgency to help the children, by praying, writing them letters, and donating school supplies and financial funds. I am looking forward to many more visits and seeing these children grow into young Christian adults. When I speak to them, I can feel and see in their eyes the hunger for the word of the gospel of Jesus Christ. I thank God for making this connection with the Golden Tots Preparatory School through Swansea First Baptist Church.

I talk to Dr. Bramwell on a regular basis. He and his wife Abigail have done an amazing job leading the Golden Tots Preparatory School. The children have excellent manners, and are very polite and well-behaved. The bar for success has been set very high, and these students have excelled from the challenge of academics and a structured daily plan. They believe in God, and have hope for the future. The Golden Tots Preparatory School is preparing each of them with the tools needed to build a successful future, while putting the Lord Jesus Christ first in all that they do.

I'm looking forward to my next visit, and sharing new fishing pictures and new personal experiences of my walk with Jesus Christ with the children. To God be the Glory!

~ *Uttermost Ministries: Dr. Ron Rowe* ~

My first trip to Kenya was filled with excitement and anticipation. After meeting Pastor Terry Wilder in 2014, I was locked in to go on my first Africa mission in September 2015 with the Swansea First Baptist mission team. It was going to be their 17th medical mission in Kenya. Pastor Terry lined up the trip and took care of all the logistics. All I had to do was raise my money, get my vaccination shots, and pack my bags.

I knew we were going to meet a good friend of his in Nairobi, Dr. Ron Rowe, but I had no idea what a huge blessing God was setting me up for.

The Africa medical mission was a huge success! We had a perfect team of 12 mission workers. Most had prior experience, so I was taught by the best. It was a humbling experience to serve the Lord, helping others with food and medicine. Sharing Jesus was so much fun! The people of Kenya were truly thirsty for the word of the Lord. The more you talked about Jesus, the more they wanted to hear.

It was during this initial trip that God planned for me to meet Dr. Ron. Dr. Ron had a vision to build 100 churches in Africa. It was during this two-week mission trip, where I was able to see the churches he had already built. For $7,000, you can build a 30' x 50' structure, with a metal roof, stone walls, and a concrete floor. It will change the lives of many people in the villages. It will not only give them a place to worship, but also a place to have meetings, weddings, medical clinics, and so much more!

After my initial Africa medical mission was under my belt, my friendship and connection with Dr. Ron grew and became stronger. Pastor Terry Wilder had a friend, Dr. Bramwell, visiting the USA for the first time in the Spring of 2016. He gave me a call and asked if I had an opening to take them fishing along with Dr. Ron. The dates worked well for my schedule, so we planned a fishing trip.

The weather was perfect for an offshore trip of 30 miles, so I took advantage of the calm seas and headed offshore. It was a successful fishing trip. There were plenty of fish! Red snapper, vermillion, and black sea bass were biting in 90' of water on live bottom. It was on the ride back to shore that Dr. Ron and I had our first conversation about me funding a church. It all sounded great, but I told him $7,000 was a lot of money. He reminded me to pray and let the Holy Spirit guide me.

The 2017 Africa medical mission came up quickly. I was ready for another trip. I had no idea what

God was planning, but I was just being obedient to His calling. I knew I was supposed to be going to Africa, but I wasn't sure what I was going to Africa for, other than to share my testimony and to share Jesus.

During this trip, I was a part of, and helped Dr. Ron Rowe dedicate his 90th church. It was powerful! Dr. Ron told me that I could do the same with $7,000. I had so many questions:

> "Who's going to build it?"
> "Where will we build it?"
> "Where will the materials come from?"

He told me to stop asking questions and just pray and let the Holy Spirit guide me.

I love maps, so I started looking at a map of Kenya. I looked at the region of Africa that we were in. The region we were in was called the Thrift Valley. It was the part of Kenya bordering Uganda. Mount Elgon was on the border. Two small villages were in the county of Trans-Nzoia, and Trans-Nzoia was in Kitale. Looking closely at Kitale, where we were staying, I noticed the county of Trans-Nzoia was the same size as the county I live in back home, Orangeburg County South Carolina. The population in Orangeburg County is approximately 100,000 people. Trans-Nzoia had 1,000,000 people. Looking closer at Trans-Nzoia, I noticed two villages, Endebess and Saboti. These villages were 17.7 kilometers apart.

When I read this, I was overcome with the Holy Spirit, and immediately realized that Endebess was similar to the town I grew up in, Norway, South Carolina, and Saboti, ten miles down the road, was similar to Bolentown, South Carolina, where I currently go to Bethany Baptist Church.

I was baptized at Norway Baptist Church in 1977 at the age of ten. I was baptized a second time at Bethany Baptist Church in 2015 at the age of 48. But it was 17.7 kilometers that gave me chills. I was born 7/17/1967 and weighed 7 pounds!

I knew immediately that I not only wanted to build one church, but I wanted to build two! I called Dr. Ron Rowe at that very moment and shared my vision.

He exclaimed, "Praise the Lord!"

"What do I have to do?" I asked.

He said, "You'll need $14,000."

I was very excited, but also knew this was a lot of money, and it would take at least two years to raise. I always tell people that I love doing business with God. Less than two months from returning from Africa in

June 2017, I had raised the $14,000 needed to fund both churches in Kenya.

Thanks to Coker Fogle, my church Bethany Baptist, and my Africa mission fund, all the money to fund the construction through Uttermost Ministries was in my hand!

Both churches were built and have been dedicated to the glory of God. Dr. Ron and I continue to build our relationship. God's plan to put us together has been an amazing journey. During our June 2019 Africa medical mission, the 100th church was dedicated. Because of Dr. Ron's obedience and faith to his vision to build these churches, God has blessed Kenya!

I look forward to continuing this journey with Dr. Ron and building another 100 churches. I can truly say that now I know why God has called me to Africa. I was called, not only to share the gospel, my testimony, and to share Jesus, but also to build churches through

Uttermost Ministries. To God be the Glory!

Pictured left to right: Pastor Terry Wilder, Captain Buddy Bizzell, Dr. Ron
Rowe (Mara River, Maasai Mara National Reserve, September 2015)

~ Endebess and Saboti: Fully Funded ~

Romans 8:28

*And we know that all things work together for good to
those who love God, to those who are the called according
to His purpose.*

Returning from my second Africa medical
mission in June 2017, I was excited to let my church,
Bethany Baptist, know the details of my trip. I'd also
contacted Norway First Baptist Church and asked to
come and speak with their members. I was invited to
speak at Norway First Baptist the following Sunday.

Norway First Baptist Church in Norway, South
Carolina, is where I was baptized in 1977, and I grew up
attending that church for most of my life. I wasn't a
regular visitor, especially during my college years or
after I got married, but I still felt a connection to this
church, and knew most of the people there.

89

I was excited to share my vision with them. I looked out into the congregation. The congregation was small in number, but very attentive. I recognized most of the faces there. I spoke about my vision to build a church in Endebess, Kenya, and name it Norway Endebess Baptist Church. I realized that this was going to be a tall task, raising $7.000 for construction. I told the congregation of mostly older people that we would raise the money through barbeque dinners, spaghetti dinners, fishing raffles, and donations. It all sounded good, but realistically we were looking at two years of fundraising.

As the service ended, I made my way to the entrance of the church to greet the people as they left. It was so good seeing all the wonderful people I remembered from my childhood. I had very good memories of Norway First Baptist.

God had a plan, and I was about to see it put into action. That last person walking out of the church was Coker Fogle. It was good seeing him. I had gone to high school with his sons, Chris and Rusty, so I had known Mr. Coker for most of my life.

As he walked up to me, he extended his right hand with a clutching grip.

He looked me in the eyes and said, "I'll give you $7,000 to build that church in Endebess, Kenya."

I was truly humbled by his generosity. My wife was by my side, and both of us were all smiles. We all went to lunch at the local restaurant, Gibson's Food Station, in Norway. During the meal, I discussed the plans and how the money would be used.

Norway Endebess Baptist Church was dedicated on the June 2019 medical mission trip. Mr. Coker wanted the dedication to honor his late wife, Margaret Anne Fogle. The scripture, Romans 8:28, and Mrs. Fogle's name, were both put on a plaque for the dedication ceremony. Due to illness, Mr. Coker passed away at the end of 2019. Because of his obedience to give, Endebess has a church. God kept Mr. Coker on earth long enough to see this vision come to pass.

The following Sunday at my church, Bethany Baptist, during the beginning of church service, Pastor Jim Broad asked if there were any announcements. I stood on the back row and announced my vision to build two churches in Kenya. I told the congregation I needed $3,500 to complete the $7,000 needed to build a church in Saboti, Kenya. I let them know that I already had $7,000 from Norway First Baptist to build a church in Endebess. My Africa mission fund had a $3,500 balance, so I was mailing this money Monday morning to Uttermost Ministries to start the construction on both churches.

I didn't know what the response would be, but God knew. It was an instant blessing! The following Sunday, the members took up an offering of $2,200, and the church matched the rest to fund the remaining $3,500 needed to construct both churches.

Within a month of returning from Kenya in June 2017, I had $14,000 to send to Uttermost Ministries. Both churches have been built, and were dedicated in June 2019. I dedicated Saboti Bethany Baptist Church to my wife and daughter. The scripture I chose was Matthew 4:19.

Matthew 4:19

Then He said to them, "Follow Me, and I will make you fishers of men."

I love doing business with God! Once I got a

taste of His Grace and Mercy, I have been on fire for

more. To God be the Glory!

~ *McDonald's Happy Meal* ~

Whenever I would go through the drive-thru at McDonald's, I would ask the cashier for the amount of the order in the vehicle directly behind me. My limit was $10, and if the amount was below, or at my limit, I would pay for their meal. I would give the cashier my business card for Edisto Palmetto Charters with my info on it, and on the back of the card, I would write, "God Bless...Captain Buddy B." This was an awesome way to be a blessing to others, as well as hand out my business cards.

Over a period of time, I would also pick my little girl up from school, and take her to McDonald's for a Happy Meal. She had seen my routine many times over.

One day, when my daughter was eight years old, she said, "Daddy, you're just throwing our money away."

"No sweetie," I said, "I'm handing out my business cards. It's called advertising, and it makes people smile. Watch the lady behind us when she finds out we paid for her meal."

As I pulled up to the window to pay for our Happy Meal, I asked about the meal price of the vehicle behind me. The cashier said the total was $12. It was a little over my limit, but I decided to pay the $12 anyway, and gave the clerk my business card to pass along to the lady. I told my daughter to watch her big smile when she gets the business card and finds out she had been blessed with a free meal.

We pulled up to the next window, both looking in anticipation. I was looking in the rearview mirror and saw exactly what my little girl had seen. The lady accepted my card and the free food, throwing my card over on the passenger seat with no smile or gratitude or appreciation. I was shocked!

My little girl said, "See Daddy? She wasn't so thankful. You're just throwing our money away."

I responded in a not so sure way, "Honey, maybe she is just having a bad day."

On the way home, I continued to try to understand how someone could be so ungrateful after receiving such a nice blessing.

It had been raining most of the day, so the roads were wet and moist. I turned into our driveway and stopped. My usual routine was to go across our busy Highway 321 and get the mail from our mailbox.

As I got out and shut the door, I looked down. There was a $1 bill folded neatly, laying on the ground at my feet. I picked it up. There was another...and another! My little girl rolled down the window, and asked me what I was doing.

I said, "Picking up money."

"I want to pick up money," she said.

"No! Stay in the truck," I laughed.

I ended up picking up 19 one-dollar bills and a five-dollar bill for a total of $24. When I walked into my home and laid it out on the counter to dry, my wife came home from work and immediately asked why all this money was on the counter.

I said, "God sent it."

I told her the story, and mentioned how it didn't make sense for this lady to be so ungrateful, so God gave me back my $12 plus $12 more.

What an awesome lesson of faith demonstrated in front of my little girl. Always be a blessing to others, because God will provide to His children. Always be positive and kind. Be the Light when there seems to be no Light.

Shortly after this, I stopped by a local family owned burger joint. I noticed a very nice, almost brand new, 18-wheeler parked outside. My little girl and I went inside and ordered two hotdogs and fries to-go.

As we sat and waited for our order, there was only one customer inside eating during this time. I mentioned to her that the 18-wheeler outside was a beautiful rig.

She said, "Thank you. I'm the owner and it's paid for."

I smiled. My little girl took the opportunity to tell the nice lady that her dad does mission work in Africa.

This began the conversation of me sharing my testimony which my little girl has heard many, many times. The lady sat listening patiently, with a smile on her face. Soon after, the waitress came out with our order.

As I reached for my wallet and the waitress rang up the total, the tractor trailer lady said, "Put their meal on my ticket."

I immediately thanked her, as did my little girl, and we both walked out smiling.

My little girl was the first to speak, exclaiming,

"Wow Daddy! Somebody finally paid for our meal!"

I exclaimed, "Yes they did. What a blessing!" I

said, "See how God works?"

What a valuable lesson in life for my little girl.

Always be a blessing to others. God sees and knows all.

He will never leave you nor forsake you. He will always

provide. We just have to have faith and stay obedient to

His calling and purpose for our lives.

~ Psalms 23 ~

Psalm 23

The Lord is my shepherd;
I shall not want.
He makes me to lie down in green pastures;
He leads me beside the still waters.
He restores my soul;
He leads me in the paths of righteousness For His name sake.
Yea though I walk through the valley of the shadow of death,
I will fear no evil;
For You are with me;
Your rod and Your staff, they comfort me.
You prepare a table before me in the presence of my enemies;
You anoint my head with oil;
My cup runs over.
Surely goodness and mercy shall follow me
All the days of my life;
And I will dwell in the house of the Lord
Forever.

During the six hours of spiritual warfare, I was not alone. My friend, Allen Fanning, and his son Braxton, were by my side the entire time. There was a battle for my soul between God and the devil. God was breaking the chains of the many strongholds of evil over my life.

During this battle, I alternated between going up and down on my knees, crying out for God to place His hand on my back and wrap His arms around me, and standing and quoting the 23rd Psalms. It was as if something had two hands around my neck and was choking the life out of me. Each time I felt the choking, I would fall back to my knees and cry out for God's help.

I cried out to Allen and Braxton to help me repeat the 23rd Psalms. As we said the passage over and over, the evil would release from me and I could stand. I went up and down like this for six hours. Allen and Braxton stood by my side as this battle took place. I noticed that when we would say the 23rd Psalms with more power and conviction, the evil seemed to release me quicker and quicker. Eventually, daybreak came.

When I walked out of the house, the sky and the trees looked different. I felt like the world had been lifted from my shoulders. I had a new heart. I was a new creation in Christ.

Not until just a few years ago, I asked God, "Why did you have me repeat the 23rd Psalms over and over that night? Out of all the scriptures in the Bible, why that one?" When I was on my knees going through six hours of spiritual warfare, I, along with my two friends, had repeated this scripture over 1,000 times.

Around 2018, I was asked to teach my Sunday School class at Bethany Baptist. This wasn't my first time teaching Sunday School, but this time, I had to prepare a lesson plan. I always look forward to teaching a lesson by digging deeply into the scripture. This time was no different.

I started preparing for the lesson the same way I always did. I prayed to God to give me guidance, and to send the message through the Holy Spirit that He wanted me to teach. Just like clockwork a message was

on my heart...the 23rd Psalms.

As I began to prepare my lesson on the 23rd

Psalms, God revealed to me that everything in this

passage of scripture had happened to me:

Psalms 23: 1

~ The Lord is my shepherd; I shall not want ~

Following the Lord has given me a peace and comfort in my life that I've never known. God knows our needs even before we ask Him in prayer. He has provided and continues to provide my every need as I serve Him daily.

I love doing business with God because He always shows out when He shows up. My need for $14,000 to build two churches was accomplished within weeks of trying to raise funds. I remember one morning, in 2015, I woke up worried about the money I needed for the plane ticket to Kenya. $1,800 was due by the end of the week, and I was short on cash. I received a $500 donation from a total stranger, Mac Hamilton, then $800 from a close friend, Ray Lovett.

Within 24 hours of waking up worried, God sent me $1,300 toward my plane ticket to Kenya. I've never been concerned about raising money for mission work since this happened.

I truly believe with all my heart that when God calls you, He will also provide for all your needs, as well as give you His full protection.

Psalms 23: 2

~ He makes me to lie down in green pastures; He leads me beside the still waters ~

This verse of scripture makes me think of a good peaceful night of sleep. There was a time though, when I was not able sleep peacefully in my home. A few months after my redemption, I was being harassed and awakened in the middle of the night by something evil. I could feel its presence laying on top of me.

I told a friend at work about the presence. She is a devout Christian, and she immediately advised me to get my home blessed. In the meantime, she said, I could command the evil spirit to leave my home in the name of Jesus Christ, and it would flee within a few nights.

The next time I went to sleep, I was awakened again, but this time, I was firmly commanding the evil spirit to leave my home in the name of Jesus Christ. And it left!

The next morning, I asked my pastor, Steve Scott, to come and bless my home. Pastor Steve showed up at my house with a new bottle of extra virgin olive oil. It was his first time being at my home, so he asked where I wanted to start. I told him we should start in the master bedroom. Pastor Steve told me we would anoint all the windows and doors in the home, while we repeated the scripture Isaiah 54:17, "No weapon formed against you shall prosper..."

Entering the master bedroom, Pastor Steve immediately turned to me and exclaimed, "There's something evil in here!"

I said, "Yes Sir! It's right there in that closet."

The closet was significant because the night after my redemption, I came home, and when I walked into the closet, I could feel an evil presence. So we started anointing my home in this very closet. Over the next two weeks, all was back to normal. Or so I thought.

One morning, I had come home after working the night shift. Trying to sleep during the daytime hours can be difficult, so I closed the blinds to my bedroom windows around 9 a.m. I was then awakened by a red cardinal tapping at my window. It was a very annoying sound. I even went out on the porch to scare it away, but that didn't work.

I was getting frustrated, then I remembered that when cardinals see their reflection in a window, it causes them to think their reflection is another bird, and then they attack their own reflection.

I opened the blinds, so that the cardinal's reflection would disappear, and I could get some sleep. When I opened the blinds, a ray of light from the sun hit the closet, lighting it up.

Wow! I couldn't believe what I was seeing! What displaces darkness? Light! When the light hit the darkened closet, the darkness was gone. The cardinal flew away, and my rest in my home has been peaceful ever since.

Psalms 23: 3

~ He restores my soul; He leads me in the paths of righteousness For His name's sake ~

Before my redemption, my will to live was gone. I did not feel worthy or loved. After six hours of spiritual warfare, God won the battle for my soul. He broke the strongholds of evil in my life. I felt love for the very first time.

He restored my soul. I wanted to live, but I knew I wanted to live for Him. He brought me along slowly. Spiritually, I had to crawl before I could walk. I had to walk before I could run, and I had to drink milk, before I could eat meat and potatoes.

Early in my journey as a Christian, God began removing people from my inner circle who meant me no good, and replaced them with godly people. My daily walk is for good, with good intentions to produce much fruit. My desire is to share Jesus at every opportunity God gives me. I never know when this opportunity will come, but I'm always ready for the assignment.

Returning to Steamboat Landing from a fishing charter one day, I came upon a distressed young lady at the dock. She was surrounded by several people who had been fishing and crabbing, and they all had stopped to help her. I didn't know what was going on, so I asked the lady.

She turned and said, "It's my birthday. I'm 40 years old. I came down to the landing today to sit in my chair and enjoy this view. The wind just blew my chair into the water. My car keys and cell phone were in the drink holder. This fisherman right here was able to catch my chair with my cell phone still in the drink holder, but my keys are in the water."

I assessed the situation and saw my fishing charter crew on their way. I turned my attention back to the young lady and told her that I would get her keys. She looked at me stunned.

It was high tide and the water was deep with very little current. I asked the fisherman for his rod and reel.

He smiled and asked, "So you're going to get the keys with this?"

I said, "No, I just want to see how deep the water is."

Everyone laughed. I used his rod and reel to determine the water was between 10' and 11' deep. It was March, and the water temperature was a cold 57 degrees! I knew I could only stay in the water a short period of time. I made a homemade rope ladder and attached it to the dock, so I could climb out of the water. I jumped into the water and it took my breath away! It was very cold!

After several attempts of diving, I found the keys! Screams of joy came from this young lady.

"I'll pay you!" she exclaimed.

"No," I said, "I don't want any money. All I want is for you to listen to my testimony."

I climbed out of the water, dried off, and shared my testimony to the young lady from Columbia, South Carolina, along with several other people fishing and crabbing on the dock.

God led me to this lady in need, and I was willing to share the gospel and give Him all the glory. I have become a willing vessel for God and He leads me in the paths of righteousness for His name sake.

Psalms 23: 4

~ Yea, though I walk through the valley of the shadow of death, I will fear no evil; For You are with me; Your rod and Your staff, they comfort me ~

II Timothy 1:7

For God has not given us a spirit of fear, but of power and of love and of a sound mind.

To fear God is the beginning of wisdom. I fear God! My first trip to Kenya in 2015 was an awesome experience. My family was worried about Ebola, terrorism and the hostile environment I would be exposed to. My answer to them was that I was afraid of what would happen to me if I didn't go to Africa. I had a burning desire to go, because this is something that God called me to do.

The first resistance I experienced was in the mountains of West Pokot, Kenya. There was a two-rut dirt road that separated the Christians and the Muslims. We stopped within a quarter of a mile of our destination. Traveling in four white vans, my team of 12 missionaries was asked to walk the last quarter of a mile through the village on this dirt road. We were walking the rest of the way, to show the Muslim community that we were not afraid, and would not be intimidated.

As we started walking, a huge Muslim mosque became visible near the road. As we approached the mosque, we were being threatened by a Muslim man, shouting at us behind the walls with a bullhorn. I was not afraid, but it felt like we might have to fight.

I remember taking my first selfie, and for a moment. I thought, this could be the last picture I ever take. After I snapped the selfie, I noticed a tall African man dressed in all red, standing closely behind me. He had a nose ring, earrings, and a painted face. He was also holding a long spear. At first, I was concerned, and as I walked towards my group, he followed me.

We eventually made it to our destination safely. Before setting up for the medical clinic, I began looking around, and could see many men dressed in red with spears. I asked Pastor Terry what was going on.

He said, "Brother, no worries. That's the West Pokot tribal community protecting us. If the Muslims had tried anything, the West Pokot tribe would have protected us."

I was amazed, but I already knew we were safe. No matter the circumstances, or how dark it may seem, God will always be there to comfort and protect His children. I've always said you cannot be an effective missionary if you're afraid. God displaced our fear with wisdom, so we would make good decisions for our well-

being, in order to serve Him better.

Psalms 23: 5

~ You prepare a table before me in the presence of my enemies; You anoint my head with oil; My cup runs over ~

Psalms 23: 6

~ Surely goodness and mercy shall follow me All the days of my life; And I will dwell in the house of the Lord Forever. ~

I've always dreamed of being a captain, and taking people fishing. I was inspired over the years by seeing others succeed at making a living doing this. God is allowing me to live my dream! There is no other place in my life where His goodness and mercy have excelled beyond my expectations and dreams.

He redeemed my life and broke the strongholds that were in the way of His plans for me. My way of achieving this dream was full of fear. Because of the strongholds of alcohol, and the fear of failure, I was unable to live my dream of being a charter captain.

God's mercy gave me a new vision. His goodness has allowed me to overcome my fears and succeed at my lifelong dream of being a fisherman. His way has blessed me in so many areas of my journey. I look forward to each fishing trip, because I never know who God is going to put on the boat, but it is always a blessing. He set me up to succeed in serving Him, and to share Jesus one charter at a time.

I know that my name is written in the Book of Life with the blood of the lamb. I will continue to serve Him, and share the story of my redemption on each fishing trip until my work on earth is done.

I have joy, peace, and comfort in knowing that after I catch my last fish, and share my story one last time, I will dwell in the house of the Lord forever. Thanks to God's goodness and mercy, I am living my dream without fear of failure. To God be the Glory!

It was amazing! Well, almost. I noticed that every single thing in this scripture was true concerning my walk with the Lord, except for one thing...I had never had my head anointed with oil, but that was about to change.

~ *Blessing Oil* ~

A few days after teaching the Sunday School lesson, I was working in the yard. All of a sudden, my Brother-in-Christ, Marty Wilson, drove up and jumped out of his vehicle with excitement.

He exclaimed, "Brother! I've got a blessing for you today!"

He opened a small bottle and said, "Take a smell." It had a very pleasant and sweet smell.

Marty asked, "You know what this is?"

"No," I said.

"It's blessing oil brother," Marty said, "And I'm going to bless your head with it."

I exclaimed, "Wow! Let's do it!"

He anointed my head with oil and began praying over me right there in my backyard. It was so powerful! I could feel the strong presence of the Holy Spirit flowing through us during his lengthy prayer. Marty prayed and eventually began speaking in tongues. I didn't know what he was saying, but I knew it felt good. When he finished, several minutes had gone by.

He exclaimed, "Brother! I've got to go! Love ya! Have a blessed day," and off he went.

After he left, I realized at that very moment, that God had completed the one thing from the 23rd Psalms that had not yet happened to me. There I was, standing in my backyard, realizing that I had just received an anointment of oil on my head from my Brother-in-Christ. I was humbled and at peace. My favorite part of this scripture is the last verse: And I will dwell in the house of the Lord forever.

A few weeks later, at my little girl's fifth-grade graduation ceremony, I was sharing this story with Cebrina, a good friend and co-worker of my wife. As I was reached the part of the story about getting my head anointed with oil, she turned and pulled out a bottle of blessing oil from her purse, and gave it to me. I offered to pay for it, but she insisted that God told her to give it to me. I kept the oil in my truck, not knowing what God had planned for me.

Just a few days later, in a subtle voice, God commanded me to go and anoint Steve's head with oil. It was in a very clear voice that He instructed me to do this. Steve was a member of my church, Bethany Baptist, and I only knew him from going to church over the last couple of years. Steve was a quadriplegic, who was paralyzed from diving into shallow water, and was now in the hospital. When I heard this news, I immediately went to see him and pray for him. He could only move his eyes; everything else was paralyzed.

Steve, by this time, had been in the hospital for over eight months. He was no longer close to Columbia, South Carolina, but had been moved to Macon, Georgia, which was three-and-a-half hours away.

I decided that I would eventually go to visit Steve, but I would have to plan an all-day trip since the round trip would be over seven hours. I even asked a couple of close friends to go with me, and both agreed to go, and told me to just let them know a date and a time.

I continued with my busy schedule of fishing for the summer, and put visiting Steve on the backburner. Once again, God spoke to me in a subtle voice, commanding me to visit Steve and anoint his head with oil, but again, I did not obey.

Shortly after summer, in September, my fishing schedule slowed down, and I was attending Sunday school at Bethany Baptist. My pastor, Jim Broad, was teaching a lesson to about ten of us. At the beginning of the lesson, Mrs. Beth, sitting next to me, asked about Steve's well-being and condition. Pastor Jim's report was not good.

Almost immediately, I felt the presence of the Holy Spirit and God's voice saying, "Go anoint Steve's head with oil."

At the end of Sunday school, I stayed behind and spoke with Mrs. Beth, sharing my calling from God to visit Steve and anoint his head with oil.

I left the Sunday school fellowship hall, and entered church for the worship service. By this time, the church was fairly full with approximately 80 or so people. My wife was sitting on the left side, halfway from the altar, but I noticed my 18-year-old nephew on the back pew, so I decided to sit by him.

The service started with a baptismal and a few songs. The deacons walked to the front of the church to begin the offering ceremony. After the offertory prayer, everyone was seated.

Immediately, when I sat on the pew, God spoke to me in a firm and very commanding voice, "Go anoint Steve's head with oil!"

I jumped to my feet, ran into the aisle, busted through the deacons taking up the offering, and found my way to my wife. As I sat by her side, I explained that God had been calling me to go visit Steve and anoint his head with oil, but I had not been obedient. This time, His voice was more firm, and I had to go.

She asked, "Ok, but after church, right?"

I said, "No, right now."

She understood, and said, "I'll see you when you get home."

I left church and found my way to Steve's girlfriend's house. Her daughter was the only one home, but she gave me the directions I needed to find Steve in Macon, Georgia.

Off I went, after entering the address in my GPS. Within 30 minutes of my arrival, I was talking to God, asking His direction on what to say and do. I did not feel worthy to anoint anyone's head with oil. I didn't know what I was supposed to say to Steve. I asked God for His guidance...to show me a sign or something.

I reached for the radio knob to turn it on. It was exactly 3 p.m. when I turned it on, and the messenger said, "Welcome to our Christian radio station program. Today's message is about being obedient to God." They began talking about scriptures in the Bible that tell us of examples of being obedient to the calling of God.

Immediately, I was overcome with tears of emotion! I knew I had not listened to God for three months. He had repeatedly asked me to visit Steve and anoint his head with oil, but I only made up excuses and did not obey Him. I cried for the next ten miles. The presence of the Holy Spirit was overwhelming. When I collected my emotions, God told me what to tell Steve.

I was to tell Steve, "You will walk again one day, either on this earth, or into the arms of Jesus." I arrived to the hospital shortly afterward.

I found Steve in a room alone. He had lost half his body mass, and could still only move his eyes. As I reached his side, I looked at him. I first apologized for not coming three months earlier, but I told him it was not too late, and that I had finally obeyed God's command. I told him, as I was guided by the Holy Spirit, that God did not do this to him, and that he was not to blame God for his condition. I prayed over him and anointed his head with oil. I reassured him not to worry about his family, because they would be taken care of.

As I walked out of the room, two nurses met with me, asking if I was a pastor.

I said, "No, I'm only a child of God who was finally being obedient to God's command."

I told them that I was at peace now, and that Steve would one day walk on this earth again, or he'd walk into the arms of Jesus.

On the way home, I called to share the story with my wife, and then my pastor. It felt really good knowing that I had finally done what God wanted me to do. I was at peace. My pastor asked if he could share my story with the congregation that Sunday evening. I was honored. I was also humbled.

Two weeks later, my pastor sent me an early morning text that said, "Steve walked into the arms of Jesus last night."

There was no more pain and no more suffering for Steve. It was a moment of relief to know that Steve was in a better place. Thank you God for using me. To God be the Glory!

~ Mr. Tommy Gibson ~

In March 2018, I was returning home from a fishing charter on Edisto Island. It was about 7 p.m in the evening, and I was tired and ready to take a shower and go to bed.

As I passed through the town of Norway, South Carolina, only five miles from my home, the Holy Spirit spoke to me in a subtle voice and said, "Go ask Tommy Gibson to build a church in Kenya."

This was a very distinct and obvious voice, and I knew I was supposed to obey and do what I was commanded to do.

However, I openly responded, "But God, it's late and I'm tired. I'll see him next Monday because I am speaking at his church's Men's Ministry."

The following Monday evening, I arrived at the Two Mile Baptist Church fellowship hall, where I was the guest speaker. I was looking forward to sharing my story, but I was also anxious to speak with Mr. Tommy Gibson. I grew up in a small town, and I went to high school with his children. Tommy's son was my age, and we had graduated high school together. Tommy Gibson was an icon, and a well-known, successful businessman in Norway. Over the years, he has given back to the community in many ways. He is also a strong and humble man of God.

As I walked into the fellowship hall, I immediately spotted Tommy in the back of the kitchen, helping to prepare the meal. I made my way through the crowd of about thirty men, and headed toward Tommy. Most of the men were local, and we all knew one another. I had not seen Tommy in a long time, so I was anxious to speak with him.

I walked up to him, and immediately said, "Good to see ya. How ya doing?" He said he was doing well.

I said, "Mr. Tommy, God told me to tell you that you can build a church in Africa for $7,000. You can name it Two Mile Baptist, and dedicate it to your family."

He said, "I will think about it, but I don't want any recognition." I told him to pray about it and let the Holy Spirit guide him.

Six months went by. It was September 2018, and I had just finished another successful summer of fishing on Edisto Island. All the kids were back in school, and my charter business had slowed to a crawl. It was time to catch up on the things around the house that needed to be done.

I received a phone call from a man named Tank Walker. Tank was calling for information about a fishing charter. He said he was a deacon at Parksville Baptist Church near McCormick, South Carolina, and they wanted to give their pastor, Craig McDaniel, a fishing trip for his birthday. I gave him the information, and told him to have Pastor Craig call me on Monday.

When I got off the phone, the Holy Spirit said, "Go talk to Mr. Tommy Gibson."

I immediately called his home, and ended up tracking him down after hours at his local restaurant. It had been six months since I last spoke with Tommy. I sat down and talked to him about our previous conversation six months earlier.

After a few questions and good fellowship, Tommy said, "Come by the office in the morning, and I'll give you a check."

I shouted, "Praise the Lord!" I asked about the recognition, and he said he wanted no recognition.

"I've done my part," he said. "Now it's between you and God to do your part."

Hope Baptist Church was built in Kitale, Kenya, in 2019, and dedicated to the people there, thanks to the generous blessing from Mr. Tommy Gibson.

~ *Pastor Craig McDaniel* ~

I met Pastor Craig McDaniel after he received a gift from his church, a $450 half-day fishing trip. The following Monday, he called to schedule a date. During the conversation, he asked what I was doing Friday night, and if I could come to his Men's Ministry to share my story. I was humbled, and told him I'd be there, and that I looked forward to the fellowship.

Friday night, at Parksville Baptist Church, I shared my story. I brought along a good friend, Steve Seigler, to be my time keeper. I wanted him to stop me once I'd reached 25 minutes. I may have gone a little over that time, but it was all good, as was the fellowship and the food.

A week before the scheduled fishing trip, Pastor Craig called and asked a few more questions about the fishing trip, but mainly, he wanted to know about building a church in Africa. I was excited to share the information with him. He said Deacon Tank Walker was convicted with the Holy Spirit to seek this information, and that the church could afford the $7,000 price. I told him we would talk more on our fishing trip.

We had a successful fishing trip. We talked about the work of Dr. Ron Rowe and Uttermost Ministries to build 100 churches in Africa. Pastor Craig took this information, and after consulting with Dr. Ron Rowe, he presented it to his church. Parksville Baptist, a 179-year-old church, had never ventured into the mission field in other countries, so this was a huge step for the church.

Pastor Craig was optimistic and asked me to keep his church in prayer as they voted. Soon after the church meeting, Pastor Craig called me with the awesome news! They wanted to build a church, as well as pay for his trip to Kenya the following summer, if he could go. I was excited and welcomed him to the 2019 Africa Medical Mission team.

The June 2019 Medical Mission with Pastor Terry Wilder of Swansea First Baptist Church was a huge success. During our two-week trip, Pastor Craig and I were able to visit 11 churches. During these visits, Parksville Mt. Emmaus Baptist was dedicated.

Our journey continues, as God has teamed us up together to serve Him by building churches in Kenya. Through the obedience of a few people, Parksville Baptist Church has a mission field in Kenya through Mt. Emmaus to support and serve.

~ Games of the World ~

Hebrews 13:2

Do not forget to entertain strangers, for by so doing some have unwittingly entertained angels.

Back in the day, I would love to gamble on college football. Gradually I lost interest in losing my money more times than not, so I stopped.

After my redemption in May 2012, I would still buy a scratch-off lottery ticket every now and then, along with a regular lottery ticket or two. My routine with scratch-offs would be to buy a few over the work week, then scratch them all off at the end of the week.

One summer afternoon, on the ride home from work, I was listening to a sermon on the radio. The message was titled, "Don't get caught up in the games of the world." I looked over in the passenger seat, and there was one scratch-off that was valued at $200,000 if you won. When I picked it up, I was convicted with the Holy Spirit not to gamble anymore. It was a strong conviction. I knew at that moment, I would never play the games of the world again. No lottery tickets. No scratch-offs. Nothing.

As I headed home, through the town of Williston, South Carolina, I asked God to show me someone to give this last scratch-off ticket to. I didn't want to throw it away. I pulled into the local grocery store parking lot to use the ATM. Getting out of my SUV, I noticed an elderly black woman sitting on a green bench on the bike path reading a book. I paused and glared her way for only a moment.

After getting some money, I went down the street for some gas and a drink. As I pulled out of the gas station, I decided to ride back to where the lady was sitting on the bench. I pulled up, leaving my SUV running, and my door open. I walked up to her.

As she looked up, I could see there was a big Bible in her lap. I said hello, and offered her the scratch-off, for a chance to win $200,000.

She took the ticket, momentarily pausing, then handed it back to me and said, "No thanks."

I was surprised. Why didn't she take this free opportunity to win some money? I immediately asked her to wait for a second while I ran to turn my vehicle off. I came back and sat beside her on the bench and introduced myself. She also introduced herself as a retired school teacher, who often came to this location daily to read her Bible.

I asked her, "Why didn't you take the free scratch-off worth $200,000?"

She answered by asking, "Why were you giving it to me?"

I explained that I was talking to God and listening to a sermon on the radio about not playing the "games of the world". I told her that I was convicted with the Holy Spirit not to play the lottery or scratch-offs anymore. I also told her that I had asked God to show me someone to give this last scratch-off to, then He showed me her, sitting on the bench on the bike path.

As we were talking, a young teenage black boy walked by, stopping to ask if we were okay.

Looking up to him in the middle of our conversation, she smoothly said to him, "Move along son. Move along."

She turned her attention back to me and said, "Just the other day, I was watching television, and the commercial was talking about winning the lottery. I told God that I would love to win some money. I didn't need one million dollars, but $200,000 would do. But that was a test, not only for you, but for me too. I think we both passed."

I was amazed at her answer. I thanked her and headed home. Since that day, I have not gambled or played any "games of the world". Almost daily, for over a year after that day, I would pass that location, but I never did see that lady again.

One day, I stopped to speak with three guys who were locals to the area, and we spent time under an oak tree near the bench. I asked about the lady, and described her as the lady who would read her Bible daily on the bench.

I explained that I had met her over a year ago, and could not remember her name. All three guys looked at me with a puzzled face. They each said they had never seen this lady, or even knew of her. They also said they had never seen anyone sit on that green bench and read the Bible. I did not understand. I thanked them and went on my way.

I truly believe this lady was an Angel, and God used her to give me confirmation not to play the "games of the world".

~ The Dream: You Tube Preacher ~

Acts 2:17

And it shall come to pass in the last days, says God, That I will pour out of My Spirit on all flesh;

Your sons and your daughters shall prophesy, Your young men shall see visions,

Your old men shall dream dreams.

I was checking my text messages early one morning, and saw a message from Janet Garrick that read, "I had a dream about you last night. My middle-aged daughter had the same dream. You need to look up Pastor Steven Furtick and listen to the sermon, 'God didn't need Peter, He just needed his boat.'"

As I listened to the 11-minute message, I cried through it all. This message was for me! Pastor Steven Furtick's message, "Why God Chose You," was about Jesus asking Peter to borrow his boat so he could use it to preach to the multitudes on the bank of Galilee. Peter said yes, and pushed Jesus out into the water after He got into the boat.

But what if Peter had said no? What would Jesus have done? He would have walked to the next fisherman with a boat and asked to use their boat. You see...God didn't need Peter; He just needed his boat.

This message was powerful, and it humbled me. I listened to it three times, clinging to every word. God's message to me was that He only needs *my* boat; He doesn't need me. As I am obedient, God continues to use me to share the good news of Jesus Christ, one charter at a time.

Janet Garrick is a good friend. She has strong faith, so when she sent me this message, I knew that there would be a blessing for me in the message.

I pray that I remain humble each and every day I serve the Lord. He did not need me; He only needed a willing vessel. I'm excited to be a vessel that He can use! He has blessed me beyond anything I could have ever imagined or dreamed for my life. To God be the Glory!

~ *Santee Lake: The Lady and the Duck* ~

I took a weekend trip to Santee with my family and friends. It was summertime, and we took a weekend vacation on Santee Lake. After arriving and checking into the cabin late Friday evening, I decided to wait until Saturday morning to put my boat in the water, and bring it around to the dock.

Saturday morning came rather quickly, as I tossed and turned around 5 a.m. to 5:30 a.m. I was sleepless, but didn't want to get up so early. However, the Holy Spirit had other plans for me, and eventually, I got up.

I decided that there was enough daylight to put my boat in the water and bring it around to the dock. After removing my boat at the landing and parking my truck, I came back to my boat. I decided to take it out for a little test run before going to the dock.

I put on some country music and off I went, cruising across the open waters of the Santee. Almost immediately, I hit a dense fog bank. It was still before sunrise, and the early morning temperatures had caused a dense fog bank to form over this area.

I immediately slowed and turned back toward the landing, because I knew it was too dangerous. I slowly cruised towards the direction of the boat ramp and floating dock. I was dressed with a pair of flip flops, shorts, and no shirt. I could only see fog in the distance as I slowly made my way back.

Within 100 yards of the boat ramp, the fog began to lift. I could make out the floating dock and boat ramp. As I got closer, I could also see a young black lady standing on the floating dock. I drifted to the dock, tied up the boat, and lowered my music. The lady was standing and staring at several wood ducks floating around on the water's edge. I approached her and asked if she was okay.

She said, "Yes, I am fine."

"Are you sure?" I asked.

She hesitated, then with a puzzled look on her face, she said, "Well, I've been sitting at the rest area just over the bridge there since 3 a.m. talking and praying to God. I'm from the Lowcountry, and on my way to see my family in the Upstate. When I left the rest area and drove over the Santee Bridge, God told me to come to the landing when I crossed over the bridge. So I did. I have been talking and praying to God to give me some answers and direction to some family and personal problems in my life. So when I pulled up to this landing, I walked out onto this dock, all I saw was dense fog over the water and these three ducks at the water's edge. Then I heard this music, but I couldn't see anything. All of a sudden, you came out of the fog in your boat with the music blaring. When I saw you, I didn't understand what God was trying to tell me."

I smiled and said, "I have a testimony. I was redeemed less than two years ago. God gave me some visions."

After sharing my story, she shared her story and personal issues.

She told me her name, and she said, "I am a youth pastor in my church."

I shared my walk with Jesus with her. I then gave her some advice though the Holy Spirit. She also shared her story and her walk with the Lord. She gave me some advice also, and then we prayed.

I used her advice and a prayer was answered. I'll probably never see her again, but I hope my advice answered her prayers also. Sometimes God will give us the answer in unusual ways. If we seek Him, we will find Him. To God be the Glory!

~ Skin of a Rhino ~

Matthew 7:15-20

Beware of false prophets, who come to you in sheep's clothing, but inwardly they are ravenous wolves.

You will know them by their fruits. Do men gather grapes from thornbushes or figs from thistles?

Even so, every good tree bears good fruit, but a bad tree bears bad fruit.

A good tree cannot bear bad fruit, nor can a bad tree bear good fruit.

Every tree that does not bear good fruit is cut down and thrown into the fire.

Therefore by their fruits you will know them.

God has removed the people from my inner circle that did not have good intentions toward me. He has replaced them with godly people who want to see me thrive and succeed in the name of Jesus. God's plan and His choice of people has given me a purpose to live my life serving Him.

I have been talked about, lied to, shunned, ridiculed, cursed, singled out, left behind, laughed at, bullied, accused of bullying, investigated, mocked, set up for failure, turned in, falsely accused, blasphemed against, intimidated, ridiculed, blamed, and the list goes on and on. I was hanging around a lot of wolves in sheep's clothing.

When you take up the cross and follow Jesus, the world is not going to be happy for you. In fact, there will be jealousy, envy, hatred, and evil intentions toward your actions and well-being. God gives us the protection and comfort to know that He will never leave us nor forsake us.

2 Timothy 1:7

For God has not given us a spirit of fear, but of power and of love and of a sound mind.

There are three things that Pastor Steve Scott told me I needed to have in order to get behind the pulpit:

1. The heart of a child
2. The mind of a theologian
3. The skin of a rhinoceros

I truly believe these traits are also needed to be a Christian, especially the skin of a rhinoceros. I use that one often.

Stay thirsty for the Lord and don't let anyone steal your joy. Serving the Lord and doing business with Him has been an exciting journey. Each day is a new day of Grace and Mercy. I look forward to each day and the direction God takes me in. To God be the Glory!

~ My First Sermon: The Heart ~

Genesis 6:5

Then the Lord saw that the wickedness of man was great in the earth, and that every intent of the thoughts of his heart was only evil continually.

Walking with the Lord has truly been the best decision of my life. Everything is better because of my obedience. My life changed when I boarded that plane to Kenya in September 2015. I've been to over 50 churches and gatherings in the name of Jesus Christ, sharing my story. I love speaking and sharing Jesus with others. I always get a blessing in return when I share my testimony. I've also been able to hear some amazing stories of how God has changed circumstances and lives.

In January 2019, my pastor asked me to preach a sermon. He told me to pick a date and prepare a message. I was honored and humbled. We picked March 17, 2019. I had plenty of time to prepare a sermon. It was going to be my first sermon that didn't include my testimony. I immediately asked God to give me the sermon that He wanted me to share. He gave me three messages in short order. I knew I could only speak one, but all three messages had something in common...the heart. So I knew my message was going to be about the heart.

As I prepared my notes, I chose the story of Paul. Paul had an encounter with God on the road to Damascus, as he was on his way to persecute Christians. I felt a connection. God changed Paul's heart after Ananias prayed over him, and he regained his eyesight. Paul traveled over 10,000 miles over the next 30 years sharing the gospel. Only God can change your heart.

All men are born with a wicked heart. God changed my heart. He gave me a purpose to live with visions. As I've been obedient and faithful, God has blessed me. Because of God's Grace and Mercy, I am able to live the life He planned for me. Once I got a taste of His blessings and favor, I have a burning desire for more.

My first sermon opened my eyes about my new heart...the heart that God gave to me. You can also get a new heart. Just ask Jesus Christ to be your Lord and Savior, and invite Him into your heart. To God be the Glory!

~Taste of God's Favor: I love doing business with God~

John 15:5

"I am the vine, you are the branches. He who abides in Me, and I in him, bears much fruit; for without Me you can do nothing..."

Obedience and faith bring blessings and favor. God has brought me along slowly. After my redemption, I had to find my way. Like a baby first crawls, walks, and runs, I had to learn when God was speaking to me through the direction of the Holy Spirit. I wanted to stay thirsty for the Lord. I began to seek Him every day. I had to learn how to pray in the name of Jesus Christ. I had to learn how to believe when I prayed, and have faith that God would answer in His time. God answers prayers in three ways: Yes, No, and Not Yet.

I had to learn to be patient. The beginning of seeking my visions was the beginning of doing business with God. Almost immediately, God started opening doors for my good. He was also closing doors for my protection. He replaced my inner circle of friends with godly and positive people, who would positively influence my well-being. As I prayed for things and circumstances, God began to work in my life.

Proverbs 16:9

A man's heart plans his way,
But the Lord directs his steps.

God has blessed me. He has given me the title of Captain. I am able to serve Him on the boat and do what I love to do...fish! I never know who is going fishing with me, but when the phone rings, I know God is setting up the trip.

Once I got a taste of God's favor in my life, I've been seeking more of it each day. I prayed for a boat. I own the nicest boat of my life. I prayed for a truck. I'm driving the nicest truck I've ever owned. I prayed for a

home on Edisto Island. He has blessed me with a home

and my neighbor is Pastor Chic Morrison. God's favor in

my life has been overwhelming.

Jeremiah 29:11

For I know the thoughts that I think toward you, says the lord, thoughts of peace and not of evil, to give you a future and a hope.

I followed the guidance of the Holy Spirit in all

of these decisions. I put God first and prayed for His

guidance. He has lined up the people and circumstances

in my life for my good. Apart from God, we can do

nothing. To God be the Glory!

~ God has a Sense of Humor: False Teeth ~

John 3:16-20

For God so loved the world that He gave His only begotten Son, that whoever believes in Him should not perish but have everlasting life.

For God did not send His Son into the world to condemn the world, but that the world through Him might be saved.

He who believes in Him is not condemned; but he who does not believe is condemned already, because he has not believed in the name of the only begotten Son of God.

And this is the condemnation, that the light has come into this world, and men loved darkness rather than light, because their deeds were evil.

For everyone practicing evil hates the light and does not come to the light, lest his deeds should be exposed.

One day, I had been running errands in

Orangeburg for most of the morning. It was time for me

to head home and get ready for the night shift. On the

way out of town, I stopped at a gas station for gas.

When I got out of my truck to pump gas, I was

approached by a young lady. It was close to noon, so I

had picked up a couple of Thickburgers at Hardees, one for lunch and the other for work.

The young lady asked for a ride. I was trying to discern if her need was genuine. I asked her where she wanted to go.

She said, "Only a little ways down the road to the laundromat." It was on my way, so I agreed to give her a ride.

She was a petite lady with a very pretty smile. I thought this would be an excellent opportunity to share my testimony on the short ride.

After paying for the gas, we loaded up and headed toward the laundromat. I began to question her about her faith and asked her if she was saved. You could really smell the Thickburgers in the backseat by this time.

She answered all of my questions. "Yes," she said, "I am saved, but I don't go to church like I should."

I started sharing my story of redemption and it was about then that we arrived at the laundromat. I pulled into the parking lot and parked my truck. I continued sharing my story, but I couldn't help but notice that she kept looking back at my Hardees bag. The smell of those Thickburgers was overwhelming.

I reached in the backseat and grabbed the Hardees bag with two burgers and fries. I asked if she was hungry, and she said yes. As her eyes locked in on the bag, I gave her the bag, and told her that she could take it with her. I continued sharing Jesus with her. It was a powerful moment. I knew I had made a connection after she started tearing up and admitted that she had made some bad choices in her life.

I asked if I could pray for her, and she said yes. After praying, I continued to tell her how my relationship with Jesus Christ changed my life.

It was about this time that she asked, "Do you mind if I eat while you talk?"

I said, "No problem." She immediately tore into the bag and unwrapped a burger. I wasn't prepared for what happened next.

She was a beautiful young lady, with a beautiful smile, and maybe 40 years old. I really couldn't believe how hungry she was, to rip into the bag like she did.

Then, after unwrapping a Thickburger, she takes her teeth out, and places them on the center console. All of her teeth! A full set of pretty white teeth. As I stared, but continued to talk, she started eating like she was starving. God has a sense of humor and I truly believe this was a Kodak moment.

Since she was enjoying her food, I took the opportunity to share more about Jesus Christ and His love for her. I noticed after the third bite, she needed a drink, so I offered her my Diet Coke from Hardees. She took a big drink and continued eating.

Only a few moments and stories later, she was finished with her burger. She thanked me for the ride and for shedding light on her life. She gathered her things and opened the door to get out.

I looked down and said, "Please don't forget your teeth."

We both smiled. As she walked around the back of the laundromat, I sat in the truck for several minutes, thinking about what had just happened.

I love sharing Jesus and telling people about my story of redemption. I pray that if there is anyone at the crossroads, I may recognize them and witness to them, and tell them about Jesus Christ. He is the way, the truth, and the life. This encounter was no different, but it will definitely be one I will never forget.

I don't know her circumstances, but it looked like she was homeless. I pray that God waters the seed planted in her life, and she will see the light, and love the light more than the darkness.

~ *Always Share Jesus: Be Obedient* ~

Matthew 4;19

Then He said to them, "Follow Me, and I will make you fishers of men."

God has given me the perfect mission field on the Edisto Palmetto. I love sharing Jesus, one charter at a time. Just a few years ago, I was fishing with two 14-year-old boys. We were about ten miles out from shore. It was a beautiful day to be on the ocean. The fish were really hungry and making me look good. It was a four-and-a-half hour trip, and we had been fishing hard for three hours, catching plenty of fish. There were lots of laughs and memories being made.

It was getting close to the time for us to start heading back to the dock. We were 45 minutes away. When I share my testimony on a fishing trip, I never know when it will happen. Sometimes, I feel led by the

Holy Spirit to share my story of redemption at the very beginning of the trip, but each trip is different. All I know is that when my phone rings and I book a trip, that's a divine appointment from God. It's then my job to share Jesus. I always get excited on each trip for the opportunity to tell new people how my relationship with Jesus Christ changed my life.

This fishing trip was no different. A single mother booked a trip with me to take her teenage son and his friend fishing. God made the appointment, and now I had to do my part.

During the first three hours of the fishing trip, we were busy having fun and catching lots of fish. I realized that I had not yet shared my story of redemption. I started to overthink the situation. I thought, "These young boys don't want to hear my story." Then I realized it wasn't up to me to pick and choose who I witnessed to on the boat. God wants me to witness to every person I take fishing, including teenagers. I was convicted with the Holy Spirit at that very moment, and began telling my story to those young men.

As we continued to catch fish, I could tell they were focused on every word I was saying. After a short time, I finished my story. It was time to lock everything down and head back to the dock.

As I began putting everything in place for the ride back, one of the young men got my attention.

As I stopped and looked at him, he said, "Captain Buddy, I really appreciate you sharing your story. It means a lot to me. Just two years ago when I was 12 years old, my best friend died in my arms. He was playing with a gun and he accidently shot himself. He died in my arms. I couldn't go to sleep that night, so I prayed to God for help. He gave me peace and comfort to fall asleep. Thank you again for sharing your story. It means more than you think."

Wow! I was humbled. I almost didn't share my story. Never again! Never again would I try to pick and choose who I witness to on the boat. We are all God's children.

Our stories of redemption help sharpen one another. This young man sharpened me. I've learned that when I witness, there's always a message in return. It's a two-way encounter. Thank you God for choosing me to be your disciple in Africa and Captain of the Edisto Palmetto. Obedience and faith brings blessings and favor. To God be the Glory!

Matthew 7:7

Ask, and it will be given to you; seek, and you will find; knock, and it will be opened to you.

Traveling back from a weekend trip to

Tennessee with my wife and daughter, we stopped at

an exit off of I-26 near Newberry, South Carolina, to use

the restroom. I immediately noticed an SUV with the

hood up parked nearby. My family went into the store,

so I walked over to check on the couple that had broken

down.

There, I met Nancy Johnson and her husband,

Ronnie Johnson. I shared my information with them,

and they said there was a wrecker on the way to help

them. I felt like it was a divine meeting. I had just told

my wife and daughter God was slowing us down on I-26

because there was something waiting for me up ahead.

Due to a wreck on the interstate, it had taken us over an hour to go ten miles to reach that exit. I'd told my family that we would get off at the first exit because they had to go to the restroom really bad.

When we found this gas station, and I spotted the stranded SUV, I knew immediately why we were slowed down. Standing there, sharing my testimony with this awesome couple, I had no idea how I was fixing to receive a blessing.

After giving them a business card to go fishing, Nancy gave me her recently published book, which was published by SmallStories Publishing. Her book is titled, "Million Dollar Producer: From the Cotton Field to the Capital." I thanked her for the book and returned to my family in our vehicle. My wife asked about my new friends. I showed her the book and told her that it looked like I'd been talking to some wealthy and blessed people. I jokingly asked my wife to read the small paperback book, and tell me what it said, because I'm not much of a reader. She quickly let me know that it was for me to read, not her.

A few days later, I started to read the story of Nancy Johnson. I couldn't' put the book down! After reading the book, I was sharpened and inspired by her story. Soon afterward, I was talking to a co-worker, Lisa Sandifer, about the book one morning, over a cup of coffee. She told me how she had been inspired in a similar way by a book a man had given her years earlier, after she had battled cancer. She explained to me how the book gave her a purpose in life when she was seeking answers. God is always right on time!

Later that day, I was preparing a speech for my men's ministry at Bethany Baptist. As I turned to Matthew 7:7 in the Bible and began to write the words in my notes, I was overcome with the Holy Spirit. I stopped writing. All I could say was, "I'm going to write a book," over and over. I said this about ten times! I couldn't believe what I was saying, but I know that nothing is impossible with God.

Thank you Nancy Johnson! Your story has inspired me to share Jesus through my testimony and daily encounters in a book titled, "Face of the Lamb: Jesus is Always Right on Time."

I truly believe if we are in the word, and seeking the Lord continually, He will put people in our paths to bless us. Stay thirsty for the Lord. Stay alert for His blessings. Pray for discernment, and the guidance of the Holy Spirit. Be obedient and faithful. To God be the Glory!

~ Conclusion ~

John 15:16

You did not choose Me, but I chose you and appointed you that you should go and bear fruit, and that your fruit should remain, that whatever you ask the Father in My name He may give you.

I do not know why God chose me, but I am so thankful He did. Because of His Grace and Mercy, I am living God's plan for my life. I grew up as a loving young man who loved life and loved people. It wasn't that I was a bad person...I was just not living my life for God.

My daily plans were always about my personal gains, and not about how I could serve the Lord with my actions. I slowly fell into a depression of alcoholism that only God could fix. I'm so thankful that He answered my cry.

My advice to all is to seek a relationship with Jesus Christ. If you seek Him, you will find Him. Building a relationship with Jesus Christ allows you to have discernment, and to know when He calls on you to serve. As a shepherd calls His sheep, they will come because they know His voice.

If you have a relationship with Jesus, you will recognize His voice when He calls. When He calls, be obedient to your calling. When I was called to go to Africa, my life changed as soon as I got on the plane in 2015.

Being faithful and obedient brings blessings and favor. To God be the Glory!

~ About the Author ~

Captain Buddy Bizzell was raised on a farm, and brought up in a good Christian home. Baptized in 1977 at the age of ten years old, the seed was planted at an early age to serve the Lord.

His upbringing included hard work, a love of sports, and determination to succeed in life. The farm was all about making a living, from picking watermelons, cantaloupes and honeydews, to gathering bales of hay to store for winter to feed over 100 head of beef cattle. Hard work left him little time to get into trouble. He was always going to bed early and getting rest for the next day's work.

In high school, as his love of sports grew, Buddy began to play travel softball, after playing baseball, soccer and tennis. In 1983, Buddy participated in his first state soccer 2A championship for Heritage Hall Academy, where he was the starting goal keeper.

After graduating high school, Buddy attended Clemson University with his best friend from high school, Robert Fort. Buddy graduated from Clemson in 1989 with a Bachelor of Science degree in Industrial Management. His first job was working for Milliken as a Production Manager in Barnwell, South Carolina.

After less than two years on the production line in textiles, Buddy returned to the farm for a short time, eventually landing a job with the Savannah River Site (SRS) in Aiken, South Carolina, in 1992. Buddy currently works shift hours at Savannah River Nuclear Solutions (SRNS), with plans to retire in five years and fish full time.

2011 was a devastating year for Buddy, but God turned it all around for him in 2012. Captain Buddy has been obedient and faithful to his calling. He is now living God's plan for his life.

In 2014, after getting his USCG Captain's License, he started a successful fishing charter business on Edisto Island, South Carolina, where he continues to serve the Lord on the water, one guest at a time.

Captain Buddy Bizzell is happily married to his lifetime partner, Bonnie Bizzell. They have one child, Kristen, who is 13 years old and has been a blessing to their lives as they serve the Lord.

Captain Buddy Bizzell's story is still being written, but this book provides a few chapters of his life-changing experience after seeing the Face of the Lamb.

To God be the Glory!

Connect with Buddy

Phone: (803) 603-2781

Facebook: @buddybizzell

Facebook: @CaptBuddyB

YouTube: Edisto Palmetto Charters LLC Capt Buddy Bizzell

Email: buddybizzell@yahoo.com

Made in the USA
Columbia, SC
22 December 2022